SHURLEY ENGLISH

HOMESCHOOL MADE EASY

LEVEL 2

Student Book

By
Brenda Shurley

Shurley Instructional Materials, Inc., Cabot, Arkansas

03-15
Shurley English Homeschooling
Level 2 Student Workbook
ISBN 978-1-58561-045-7

Copyright © 2001 by Shurley Instructional Materials, Inc.
No part of this book may be reproduced or transmitted in any form or by any means, electronic or mechanical, including photocopying, recording, or by any information storage or retrieval system, without written permission from the Publisher.

Printed in the United States of America by RR Donnelley, Owensville, MO.

For additional information or to place an order, write to: Shurley Instructional Materials, Inc.
                                                        366 SIM Drive
                                                       Cabot, AR 72023

1 2 3 4 5 6 7 8 9 10   15 14 13 11 09 07 06 05 03 02

JINGLE

SECTION

Jingle Section

Jingle 1: Sentence Jingle

A sentence, sentence, sentence
Is complete, complete, complete
When 5 simple rules
It meets, meets, meets.

It has a subject, subject, subject
And a verb, verb, verb.
It makes sense, sense, sense
With every word, word, word.

Add a capital letter, letter
And an end mark, mark.
Now, we're finished, and aren't we smart!
Now, our sentence has all its parts!

REMEMBER
Subject, Verb, Com-plete sense,
Capital letter, and an end mark, too.
That's what a sentence is all about!

Jingle 2: Noun Jingle

This little noun
Floating around
Names a person, place, or thing.
With a knick knack, paddy wack,
These are English rules.
Isn't language fun and cool?

Jingle 3: Verb Jingle

A verb shows action,
There's no doubt!
It tells what the subject does,
Like sing and shout.

Action verbs are fun to do.
Now, it's time to name a few.
So, clap your hands
And join our rhyme;
Say those verbs
In record time!

Wiggle, jiggle, turn around;
Raise your arms
And stomp the ground.
Shake your finger
And wink your eye;
Wave those action verbs good-bye.

Jingle Section

Jingle 4: Adverb Jingle

An adverb modifies a verb, adjective, or another adverb.
An adverb asks *How? When? Where?*
To find an adverb: **Go, Ask, Get**.
Where do I **go**? To a verb, adjective, or another adverb.
What do I **ask**? How? When? Where?
What do I **get**? An ADVERB! (Clap) (Clap) That's what!

Jingle 5: Adjective Jingle

An adjective modifies a noun or pronoun.
An adjective asks *What kind? Which one? How many?*
To find an adjective: **Go, Ask, Get**.
Where do I **go**? To a noun or pronoun.
What do I **ask**? What kind? Which one? How many?
What do I **get**? An ADJECTIVE! (Clap) (Clap) That's what!

Jingle 6: Article Adjective Jingle

We are the article adjectives,
Teeny, tiny adjectives:
A, AN, THE - A, AN, THE.

We are called article adjectives and noun markers;
We are memorized and used every day.
So, if you spot us, you can mark us
With the label A.

We are the article adjectives,
Teeny, tiny adjectives:
A, AN, THE - A, AN, THE.

Jingle Section

Jingle 7: Preposition Jingle

A PREP PREP PREPOSITION
Is a special group of words
That connects a
NOUN, NOUN, NOUN
Or a PRO, PRO, PRONOUN
To the rest of the sentence.

Jingle 8: Object of the Prep Jingle

Dum De Dum Dum!
An O-P is a N-O-U-N or a P-R-O
After the P-R-E-P
In a S-E-N-T-E-N-C-E.
Dum De Dum Dum - DONE!

Jingle 9: Pronoun Jingle

This little pronoun,
Floating around,
Takes the place of a little old noun.
With a knick knack, paddy wack,
These are English rules.
Isn't language fun and cool?

Jingle 10: Subject Pronoun Jingle

There are seven subject pronouns
That are easy as can be:
I and we,   (clap 2 times)
He and she,   (clap 2 times)
It and they and you.   (clap 3 times)

Jingle 11: Possessive Pronoun Jingle

There are seven possessive pronouns
That are easy as can be:
My and our,   (clap 2 times)
His and her,   (clap 2 times)
Its and their and your.   (clap 3 times)

REFERENCE SECTION

Vocabulary Reference – Level 2

Chapter 2, Vocabulary Words #1	Chapter 2, Vocabulary Words #2
(enthusiastic, eager, gallop, crawl)	(impolite, respectful, salute, tribute)

Chapter 3, Vocabulary Words #1	Chapter 3, Vocabulary Words #2
(magnificent, splendid, brisk, sluggish)	(cautious, hasty, fly, soar)

Chapter 4, Vocabulary Words #1	Chapter 4, Vocabulary Words #2
(clumsy, graceful, often, frequent)	(dangle, suspend, modern, antique)

Chapter 5, Vocabulary Words #1	Chapter 5, Vocabulary Words #2
(vanish, disappear, mournful, delightful)	(calm, excited, annoy, irritate)

Chapter 6, Vocabulary Words #1	Chapter 6, Vocabulary Words #2
(scamper, scurry, simple, complex)	(brilliant, dull, rage, anger)

Chapter 7, Vocabulary Words #1	Chapter 7, Vocabulary Words #2
(cargo, freight, arrive, depart)	(build, collapse, overhead, above)

Chapter 8, Vocabulary Words #1	Chapter 8, Vocabulary Words #2
(weary, energetic, nibble, munch)	(gush, trickle, flicker, flash)

Chapter 9, Vocabulary Words #1	Chapter 9, Vocabulary Words #2
(expert, beginner, unchanging, constant)	(keep, abandon, immerse, plunge)

Chapter 10, Vocabulary Words #1	Chapter 10, Vocabulary Words #2
(old, youthful, canyon, gorge)	(dangerous, harmless, bewilder, confuse)

Chapter 11, Vocabulary Words #1	Chapter 11, Vocabulary Words #2
(clog, block, exhausted, refreshed)	(alert, aware, tardy, punctual)

Chapter 12, Vocabulary Words #1	Chapter 12, Vocabulary Words #2
(stride, waddle, beneath, below)	(cranky, grouchy, nimble, slow)

Vocabulary Reference – Level 2 (continued)

Chapter 13, Vocabulary Words #1	Chapter 13, Vocabulary Words #2
(deep, shallow, appear, emerge)	(stable, unsteady, collect, gather)

Chapter 14, Vocabulary Words #1	Chapter 14, Vocabulary Words #2
(begin, retire, burrow, tunnel)	(advice, counsel, junior, senior)

Chapter 15, Vocabulary Words #1	Chapter 15, Vocabulary Words #2
(contented, dissatisfied, rehearse, practice)	(crisp, soggy, performance, recital)

Chapter 16, Vocabulary Words #1	Chapter 16, Vocabulary Words #2
(coast, shore, edge, middle)	(awaited, unexpected, favorite, preferred)

Chapter 17, Vocabulary Words #1	Chapter 17, Vocabulary Words #2
(fresh, moldy, desolate, barren)	(huge, enormous, ease, effort)

Chapter 18, Vocabulary Words #1	Chapter 18, Vocabulary Words #2
(distant, remote, restless, patient)	(arrogant, proud, wide, narrow)

Chapter 19, Vocabulary Words #1	Chapter 19, Vocabulary Words #2
(shout, murmur, shelf, ledge)	(shine, sparkle, victory, defeat)

Chapter 20, Vocabulary Words #1	Chapter 20, Vocabulary Words #2
(rely, depend, clear, murky)	(relaxed, anxious, damage, injure)

Chapter 21, Vocabulary Words #1	Chapter 21, Vocabulary Words #2
(frisky, lively, whisper, howl)	(pale, colorful, thrive, flourish)

Chapter 22, Vocabulary Words #1	Chapter 22, Vocabulary Words #2
(smooth, rough, meticulous, thorough)	(stretch, shrink, question, inquire)

Chapter 23, Vocabulary Words #1	Chapter 23, Vocabulary Words #2
(lazy, industrious, assistant, helper)	(gentle, rowdy, annual, yearly)

Chapter 24, Vocabulary Words #1	Chapter 24, Vocabulary Words #2
(sweet, bitter, continuous, ceaseless)	(polite, rude, limp, hobble)

State Information for the 50 States

	Chapter	State	Capital	Postal Abbreviation
1.	C 1	Alabama	Montgomery	AL
2.	C 2	Alaska	Juneau	AK
3.	C 3	Arizona	Phoenix	AZ
4.	C 4	Arkansas	Little Rock	AR
5.	C 5	California	Sacramento	CA
6.	C 6	Colorado	Denver	CO
7.	C 7	Connecticut	Hartford	CT
8.	C 8	Delaware	Dover	DE
9.	C 9	Florida	Tallahassee	FL
10.	C 9	Georgia	Atlanta	GA
11.	C 10	Hawaii	Honolulu	HI
12.	C 10	Idaho	Boise	ID
13.	C 11	Illinois	Springfield	IL
14.	C 11	Indiana	Indianapolis	IN
15.	C 12	Iowa	Des Moines	IA
16.	C 12	Kansas	Topeka	KS
17.	C 13	Kentucky	Frankfort	KY
18.	C 13	Louisiana	Baton Rouge	LA
19.	C 14	Maine	Augusta	ME
20.	C 14	Maryland	Annapolis	MD
21.	C 15	Massachusetts	Boston	MA
22.	C 15	Michigan	Lansing	MI
23.	C 16	Minnesota	St. Paul	MN
24.	C 16	Mississippi	Jackson	MS
25.	C 17	Missouri	Jefferson City	MO
26.	C 17	Montana	Helena	MT
27.	C 18	Nebraska	Lincoln	NE
28.	C 18	Nevada	Carson City	NV
29.	C 19	New Hampshire	Concord	NH
30.	C 19	New Jersey	Trenton	NJ
31.	C 20	New Mexico	Santa Fe	NM
32.	C 20	New York	Albany	NY
33.	C 21	North Carolina	Raleigh	NC
34.	C 21	North Dakota	Bismarck	ND
35.	C 22	Ohio	Columbus	OH
36.	C 22	Oklahoma	Oklahoma City	OK
37.	C 23	Oregon	Salem	OR
38.	C 23	Pennsylvania	Harrisburg	PA
39.	C 24	Rhode Island	Providence	RI
40.	C 24	South Carolina	Columbia	SC
41.	C 25	South Dakota	Pierre	SD
42.	C 25	Tennessee	Nashville	TN
43.	C 26	Texas	Austin	TX
44.	C 26	Utah	Salt Lake City	UT
45.	C 27	Vermont	Montpelier	VT
46.	C 27	Virginia	Richmond	VA
47.	C 27	Washington	Olympia	WA
48.	C 27	West Virginia	Charleston	WV
49.	C 27	Wisconsin	Madison	WI
50.	C 27	Wyoming	Cheyenne	WY

Card Sample for State Information
1. What is the state on the front of this card? **Alabama**   2. What is the capital of Alabama? **Montgomery**   3. What is the postal abbreviation of Alabama? **AL**

Reference 1: Beginning Setup Plan for Homeschool
You should use this plan to keep things in order!

1. Have separate color-coded pocket folders for each subject.

2. Put unfinished work in the right-hand side and finished work in the left-hand side of each subject folder.

3. Put notes to study, graded tests, and study guides in the brads so you will have them to study for scheduled tests.

4. Have a paper folder to store extra clean sheets of paper. Keep it full at all times.

5. Have an assignment folder to be reviewed every day.

Things to keep in your assignment folder:

A. Keep a monthly calendar of assignments, test dates, report-due dates, project-due dates, extra activities, dates and times, review dates, etc.

B. Keep a grade sheet to record the grades received in each subject.

  (*You might also consider keeping your grades on the inside cover of each subject folder. However you keep your grades, just remember to record them accurately. Your grades are your business, so keep up with them! Grades help you know which areas need attention.*)

C. Make a list every day of the things you want to do so you can keep track of what you finish and what you have not finished. Move the unfinished items to your new list the next day.

  (*Making this list takes time, but it's your road map to success. You will always know at a glance what you set out to accomplish and what still needs to be done.*)

6. Keep all necessary school supplies in a handy, heavy-duty Ziploc bag or a pencil bag.

Reference 2: What is Journal Writing?

Journal Writing is a written record of your personal thoughts and feelings about things or people that are important to you. Recording your thoughts in a journal is a good way to remember how you felt about what was happening in your life at a particular time. You can record your dreams, memories, feelings, and experiences. You can ask questions and answer some of them. It is fun to go back later and read what you have written because it shows how you have changed in different areas of your life. A journal can also be an excellent place to look for future writing topics, creative stories, poems, etc. Writing in a journal is an easy and enjoyable way to practice your writing skills without worrying about a writing grade.

What do I write about?

Journals are personal, but sometimes it helps to have ideas to get you started. Remember, in a journal, you do not have to stick to one topic. Write about someone or something you like. Write about what you did last weekend or on vacation. Write about what you hope to do this week or on your next vacation. Write about home, school, friends, hobbies, special talents *(yours or someone else's),* or present and future hopes and fears. Write about what is wrong in your world and what you would do to "fix" it. Write about the good things and the bad things in your world.

If you think about a past event and want to write an opinion about it now, put it in your journal. If you want to give your opinion about a present or future event that could have an impact on your life or the way that you see things, put it in your journal. If something bothers you, record it in your journal. If something interests you, record it. If you just want to record something that doesn't seem important at all, write it in your journal. After all, it is your journal!

How do I get started writing in my personal journal?

You need to put the day's date on the title line of your paper: **Month, Day, Year.** Skip the next line and begin your entry. You might write one or two sentences, a paragraph, a whole page, or several pages. Except for the journal date, no particular organizational style is required for journal writing. You decide how best to organize and express your thoughts. Feel free to include sketches, diagrams, lists, etc., if they will help you remember your thoughts about a topic or an event. You will also need a spiral notebook, a pen, a quiet place, and at least 5-10 minutes of uninterrupted writing time.

Note: Use a pen if possible. Pencils have erasers and lead points that break, both of which slow down your thoughts. Any drawings you might include do not have to be masterpieces—stick figures will do nicely.

Reference 3: Alphabetical Order

Directions: Put each group of words in alphabetical order. Use numbers to show the order in each column.

Math Words	"M" Words	Farm Words	Language Words	"J" Words
_1_ 1. add	_2_ 3. melon	_2_ 5. tractor	_1_ 7. noun	_1_ 9. juice
_2_ 2. subtract	_1_ 4. meadow	_1_ 6. barn	_2_ 8. verb	_2_ 10. jump

Reference 4: Synonyms and Antonyms

Definitions: Synonyms are words that have similar, or almost the same, meanings. Antonyms are words that have opposite meanings.

Directions: Identify each pair of words as synonyms or antonyms by putting parentheses ( ) around **syn** or **ant**.

1. small, tiny | **(syn)** ant
2. gentle, kind | **(syn)** ant
3. wild, tame | syn **(ant)**

Reference 5: A Four-Step Vocabulary Plan

(1) Write a title for the vocabulary words in each chapter.
   Example: **Chapter 1, Vocabulary Words**
(2) Write each vocabulary word in your vocabulary notebook.
(3) Look up each vocabulary word in a dictionary or thesaurus.
(4) Write the meaning beside each vocabulary word.

Reference 6: A and An Choices

Rule 1: Use the word *a* when the next word begins with a consonant sound.
   (*Example: a delicious orange.*)
Rule 2: Use the word *an* when the next word begins with a vowel sound.
   (*Example: an orange.*)

Sample Sentences: Write *a* or *an* in the blanks.

1. Mary was __an__ artist.
2. Mary was __a__ talented artist.
3. Thomas sang __a__ beautiful song.
4. Thomas sang __an__ amazing song.

Level 2—Shurley English—Homeschool Edition

Reference 7: Question and Answer Flow Sentence
Question and Answer Flow Sentence: The three young lions roared loudly. 1. What roared loudly? lions - SN 2. What is being said about lions? lions roared - V 3. Roared how? loudly - Adv 4. What kind of lions? young - Adj 5. How many lions? three - Adj 6. The - A **Classified Sentence:**   A   Adj   Adj   SN   V   Adv   The three young lions roared loudly.

Reference 8: Three Kinds of Sentences and the End Mark Flows	

1. A **declarative** sentence makes a statement.
   It is labeled with a **D**.
   Example: Beth looked hungrily at the cookies.
   (Period, statement, declarative sentence)
	Directions: Read each sentence, recite the end-flow in parentheses, and put the end mark and the abbreviation for the sentence type in the blank at the end of each sentence.

2. An **interrogative** sentence asks a question.
   It is labeled with an **Int**.
   Example: Did you swim in the ocean?
   (Question mark, question, interrogative sentence)
	1. Sarah collects stamps **. D**
	   (Period, statement, declarative sentence)
	
	2. How old are you **? Int**
	   (Question mark, question, interrogative sentence)

3. An **exclamatory** sentence expresses strong feeling.
   It is labeled with an **E**.
   Example: That huge tree fell on his garage!
   (Exclamation point, strong feeling, exclamatory sentence)
	3. Our team won the race **! E**
	   (Exclamation point, strong feeling, exclamatory sentence)

Reference 9: Practice Sentence						
Labels:	A	Adj	Adj	SN	V	Adv	Adv
Practice:	**The**	**little**	**green**	**snake**	**crawled**	**away**	**quickly.**

Reference 10: Improved Sentence						
Labels:	**A**	**Adj**	**Adj**	**SN**	**V**	**Adv**	**Adv**
Practice:	The	little	green	snake	crawled	away	quickly.
Improved:	**A** (word change)	**large** (antonym)	**hissing** (word change)	**reptile** (synonym)	**slithered** (synonym)	**away** (no change)	**slowly.** (antonym)

Reference 11: Definitions for a Skill Builder Check

1. A **noun** names a person, place, or thing.

2. A **singular noun** usually does not end in *s* or *es* and means only one. (*fan, doll, brush*)
   Exception: Some nouns that end in s are singular and mean only one. (*address, mess*)

3. A **plural noun** usually ends in *s* or *es* and means more than one. (*fans, dolls, brushes*)
   Exception: Some nouns are made plural by changing their spelling. (*ox - oxen, mouse - mice*)

4. A **common noun** names ANY person, place, or thing. A common noun is not capitalized because it does not name a specific person, place, or thing. (*principal, lake*)

5. A **proper noun** is a noun that names a specific, or particular, person, place, or thing. Proper nouns are always capitalized no matter where they are located in the sentence. (*Thomas, Alaska*)

Reference 12: The Topic

The topic tells what something is about. The topic can tell what a paragraph or what a group of words is about. The topic is sometimes called the subject because it tells what something is about.

Directions for finding the topic: Write the name of the topic that best describes what each row of words is about. Choose from these topics: **Sports, Clothing, Animals, or Colors**.

(1) Sports	(2) Colors	(3) Clothing
basketball	purple	sweater
tennis	red	pants
baseball	yellow	socks
soccer	blue	shorts

Level 2—Shurley English—Homeschool Edition

Reference 13: Supporting and Non-Supporting Ideas and Sentences

Words that support the topic: In each row, cross out the one idea that does not support the underlined topic at the top.
 	
    (1)   (2)   (3)
   Animals   Food   Transportation
 	
    bear   cake   truck
    rabbit   broccoli   ~~lake~~
   hippopotamus   ~~purple~~   helicopter
    chipmunk   biscuit   boat
    ~~onion~~   potato   bus

Sentences that support the topic: Read the topic. Then, cross out the one sentence that does not support the topic.
 	
      Topic: A Furry Little Bunny
 	
  1. The bunny was covered with white fur.
  2. His tail looked like a cotton ball.
  3. ~~I like bunnies and ostriches.~~
  4. His ears were long and floppy.

Reference 14: Simple Subject, Simple Predicate, Complete Subject, Complete Predicate
1. The **simple subject** is another name for the subject. 2. The **simple predicate** is another name for the verb. 3. The **complete subject** is the subject and all the words that modify the subject. 4. The **complete predicate** is the verb and all the words that modify the verb.

Reference 15: Noun Job Chart
Directions: Classify the sentence below. Underline the complete subject once and the complete predicate twice. Then, complete the table. A Adj SN V Adv Adv The small raft drifted lazily downstream.

List the Noun Used	List the Noun Job	Singular or Plural	Common or Proper	Simple Subject	Simple Predicate
raft	**SN**	**S**	**C**	**raft**	**drifted**

Page 14 - Reference Section   Level 2 Homeschool Student Book
© SHURLEY INSTRUCTIONAL MATERIALS, INC.

Reference 16: Two-Point Paragraph Sample

Topic: **My favorite colors**
Two main points: 1. **red** 2. **brown**

Sentence #1 – <u>Topic Sentence</u> (*Use words in the topic and tell how many points will be used.*)
I have two favorite colors.

Sentence #2 – <u>2-Point Sentence</u> (*List the 2 points in the order you will present them.*)
These colors are red and brown.

Sentence #3 – <u>First Point</u>
My first favorite color is red.

Sentence #4 – <u>Supporting Sentence</u> for the first point.
I like red because it reminds me of a special patchwork quilt that my grandmother made.

Sentence #5 – <u>Second Point</u>
My second favorite color is brown.

Sentence #6 – <u>Supporting Sentence</u> for the second point.
Brown reminds me of the hot fudge brownies that Grandma used to make for me.

Sentence #7 – <u>Concluding (final) Sentence</u> (*Restate the topic sentence and add an extra thought.*)
My two favorite colors, red and brown, bring back wonderful memories of my grandmother.

<u>SAMPLE PARAGRAPH</u>

My Favorite Colors

    I have two favorite colors. These colors are red and brown. My first favorite color is red. I like red because it reminds me of a special patchwork quilt that my grandmother made. My second favorite color is brown. Brown reminds me of the hot fudge brownies that Grandma used to make for me. My two favorite colors, red and brown, bring back wonderful memories of my grandmother.

Reference 17: Writing Checklist

1. Label your writing assignment in the top right-hand corner of your page with the following information:

    A. Your Name
    B. The Writing Assignment Number. *(Examples: WA#1, WA#2, etc.)*

2. Write the title of the writing on the top of the first line.
3. Have you followed the pattern for the type of writing assigned?
   (Is your assignment a 2-point paragraph, a 3-point paragraph, a descriptive paragraph, or a letter?)
4. Do you have complete sentences?
5. Have you capitalized the first word and put an end mark at the end of every sentence?
6. Have you checked your sentences for other capitalization and punctuation mistakes?
7. Have you checked for misspelled words and incorrect homonym choices?
8. Have you indented each paragraph?

Reference 18: How to Find a Preposition and an Object of the Preposition

SN   V
*Matthew fell **down the steps**.*

To find a preposition, find the word with a noun after it. The word **down** has the noun **steps** after it. Now, it is time to ask the question *What* or *Whom*. We will ask *What* since the noun is a thing and not a person: **Down what? steps** – object of the preposition.

Now, we know that the word **down** is a preposition because it has the noun **steps** (the object of the preposition) after it. To find the preposition and object of the preposition in the Question and Answer Flow, say:

Down – Preposition
Down what? steps – Object of the Preposition

Reference 19: Knowing the Difference Between Prepositions and Adverbs

    SN   V   Adv   SN   V   P   A   OP
*1. Matthew fell **down**.*   *2. Matthew fell **down the steps**.*

In the <u>first sentence</u>, *Matthew fell **down***, the word **down** is an adverb because it does not have a noun after it.

In the <u>second sentence</u>, *Matthew fell **down the steps***, the word **down** is a preposition because it has the noun **steps** (an object of the preposition) after it.

Remember, to find the preposition and object of the preposition in the Question and Answer Flow, say the words below.

Down – Preposition
Down what? steps – Object of the Preposition

Reference 20: Homonym Chart

Homonyms are words that sound the same but have different meanings and different spellings.

1. **capital** - upper part, main	15. **lead** - metal	29. **their** - belonging to them
2. **capitol** - statehouse	16. **led** - guided	30. **there** - in that place
3. **coarse** - rough	17. **no** - not so	31. **they're** - they are
4. **course** - route	18. **know** - to understand	32. **threw** - did throw
5. **council** - assembly	19. **right** - correct, opposite of left	33. **through** - from end to end
6. **counsel** - advice	20. **write** - to form letters	34. **to** - toward (a preposition)
7. **forth** - forward	21. **principle** - a truth/rule/law	35. **too** - denoting excess
8. **fourth** - ordinal number	22. **principal** - chief/head person	36. **two** - a couple
9. **its** - possessive pronoun	23. **stationary** - motionless	37. **your** - belonging to you
10. **it's** - it is	24. **stationery** - paper	38. **you're** - you are
11. **hear** - to listen	25. **peace** - quiet	39. **weak** - not strong
12. **here** - in this place	26. **piece** - a part	40. **week** - seven days
13. **knew** - understood	27. **sent** - caused to go	41. **days** - more than one day
14. **new** - not old	28. **scent** - odor	42. **daze** - a confused state

Directions: Underline the correct homonym.

1. Jennifer learned to (right, **write**) with her left hand.
2. Contestant number two had the (**right**, write) answer.

Reference 21: Subject-Verb Agreement Rules

Rule 1: A singular subject must use a singular verb form that ends in **s**: *is, was, has, does,* or verbs ending with **es**.

Rule 2: A plural subject, a compound subject, or the subject **YOU** must use a plural verb form that has **no s** ending: *are, were, do, have,* or verbs without **s** or **es** endings. (A plural verb form is also called the *plain form.*)

Directions: For each sentence, do these four things: (1) Write the subject. (2) Write **S** if the subject is singular or **P** if the subject is plural. (3) Write the rule number. (4) Underline the correct verb in the sentence.

Subject	S or P	Rule	
kitten	S	1	1. The **kitten** (**licks**, lick) his paws.
pie and cake	P	2	2. The **pie** and **cake** (**are**, is) in the oven.
You	P	2	3. **You** (watches, **watch**) for the deliveryman.

Reference 22: Singular and Plural Points

Two-Point Expository Paragraph
Topic: My favorite desserts
2-points: 1. chocolate cakes   2. peach cobblers

    I have two favorite desserts. These desserts are chocolate cakes and peach cobblers. My first favorite dessert is a chocolate cake. I like chocolate cakes loaded with lots of sugary frosting. My second favorite dessert is a peach cobbler. I love cobblers made with fresh peaches picked from my grandfather's orchard. I enjoy eating all kinds of desserts, but my favorites will always be chocolate cakes and peach cobblers.

Reference 23: Subject Pronoun

1. A **subject pronoun** takes the place of a noun that is used as the subject of a sentence.
2. These are the most common subject pronouns: *I, we, he, she, it, they,* and *you.*
   Use the Subject Pronoun Jingle to remember the common subject pronouns.
3. To find a subject pronoun, ask the subject question *who* or *what.*
4. Label a subject pronoun with an **SP**.
5. Call the **SP** abbreviation a subject pronoun.

Reference 24: Capitalization Rules

1. Capitalize the first word of a sentence.
2. Capitalize the pronoun I.
3. Capitalize the names of people and the names of pets. (*Alan, Molly*)
4. Capitalize titles used with people's names and people's initials. (*Ms., Uncle, Dr., T. S.*)
5. Capitalize names of streets, cities, states, and countries. (*Main Street, Atlanta, Georgia, Germany*)
6. Capitalize the days of the week and the months of the year. (*Friday, April*)

Sample: Correct the capitalization mistakes and put the rule number above each correction.

   1(or 3)   2   5   6   (capitalization rule numbers)
     S   I   O   T
1. sarah and i drove to ohio on tuesday.   (Editing Guide: 4 capitalization mistakes)

Level 2—Shurley English—Homeschool Edition

Reference 25: Possessive Pronouns

1. A possessive pronoun takes the place of a possessive noun.

2. A possessive pronoun's spelling form makes it possessive. A possessive pronoun does NOT contain an apostrophe. These are the most common possessive pronouns: *my, our, his, her, its, their,* and *your.* Use the Possessive Pronoun Jingle to remember the most common possessive pronouns.

3. A possessive pronoun's main job is to show ownership. (*Her kite*)

4. Use the abbreviation PP (possessive pronoun).

5. Include possessive pronouns when you are asked to identify pronouns, possessives, or adjectives.

6. To find a possessive pronoun, begin with the question *whose*. (*Whose kite? Her - PP*)

Reference 26: Punctuation Rules

1. Use a period after initials. (*J. M. Scott*)
2. Use a period after an abbreviation. (*Dr., Mrs., Oct.*)
3. Use a comma to separate the city from the state. (*Nashville, Tennessee*)
4. Use a comma between the day and the year. (*December 25, 2002*)
5. Put an end mark at the end of a sentence. (*period, question mark, or exclamation mark*)

Directions: Correct the capitalization and punctuation mistakes for the sentence below. Write the rule numbers above the capitalization corrections and below the punctuation corrections.

<u>1(or 4) 4 4 3   5   5   </u>(capitalization rule numbers)
    M   R L T   C   O

1. ms. r. l. thompson called her sister in columbus, ohio. (**Editing Guide: 6 capitals & 5 punctuation**)
<u>   2 1 1   3   5   </u>(punctuation rule numbers)

Reference 27: Possessive Nouns
1. A possessive noun is the name of a person, place, or thing that owns something.
2. A possessive noun will always have an apostrophe after it. It will be either an *apostrophe s ('s)* or an *s apostrophe (s')*. The apostrophe makes a noun show ownership. (*Tyler's camera*)
3. A possessive noun's main job is to show ownership or possession.
4. Use the abbreviation **PN** (possessive noun).
5. Include possessive nouns when you are asked to identify possessive nouns or adjectives. Do not include possessive nouns when you are asked to identify regular nouns because of their special job.
6. To find a possessive noun, begin with the question *whose*. (*Whose camera? Tyler's - PN*)

Reference 28: Making Nouns Possessive		
1. For a singular noun - add (**'s**)	2. For a plural noun that ends in **s** - add (**'**)	3. For a plural noun that does not end in **s** - add (**'s**)
Rule 1: girl's	Rule 2: girls'	Rule 3: women's

Use the following guidelines to make each noun possessive. First, identify each noun as singular or plural by writing **S** or **P** in the first blank. Next, write the correct rule number from the list above in the second blank. Finally, write the possessive form of each noun as singular possessive or as plural possessive.

Noun	S-P	Rule	Singular Possessive	Plural Possessive
1. pelican	S	1	pelican's	
2. students	P	2		students'
3. Ashley	S	1	Ashley's	
4. firemen	P	3		firemen's

Reference 29: Two- and Three-Point Expository Paragraph Guidelines	
2-Point Expository Paragraph Guidelines	**3-Point Expository Paragraph Guidelines**
Paragraph (7 sentences)	Paragraph (9 sentences)
A. Topic sentence	A. Topic sentence
B. A two-point sentence	B. A three-point sentence
C. A **first-point sentence**	C. A **first-point sentence**
D. A **supporting** sentence for the first point	D. A **supporting** sentence for the first point
E. A **second-point sentence**	E. A **second-point sentence**
F. A **supporting** sentence for the second point	F. A **supporting** sentence for the second point
G. A concluding sentence	G. A **third-point sentence**
	H. A **supporting** sentence for the third point
	I. A concluding sentence

Reference 30: Three-Point Expository Paragraph Example

Topic: **My favorite animals**
Three main points: 1. **frogs**   2. **koalas**   3. **whales**

Sentence #1 – <u>Topic Sentence</u> (*Use words in the topic and tell how many points will be used.*)
I have three favorite animals.

Sentence #2 – <u>3-Point Sentence</u> (*List the 3 points in the order you will present them.*)
These animals are frogs, koalas, and whales.

Sentence #3 – <u>First Point</u>
My first favorite animal is a frog.

Sentence #4 – <u>Supporting Sentence</u> for the first point
I like frogs because they are so funny when they hop around.

Sentence #5 – <u>Second Point</u>
My second favorite animal is a koala.

Sentence #6 – <u>Supporting Sentence</u> for the second point
I like koalas because they are excellent tree climbers.

Sentence #7 – <u>Third Point</u>
My third favorite animal is a whale.

Sentence #8 – <u>Supporting Sentence</u> for the third point
I think whales are enormous ballerinas in the water.

Sentence #9 – <u>Concluding (final) Sentence</u> (*Restate the topic sentence and add an extra thought.*)
My three favorite animals are very fascinating creatures.

SAMPLE PARAGRAPH

My Favorite Animals

    I have three favorite animals. These animals are frogs, koalas, and whales. My first favorite animal is a frog. I like frogs because they are so funny when they hop around. My second favorite animal is a koala. I like koalas because they are excellent tree climbers. My third favorite animal is a whale. I think whales are enormous ballerinas in the water. My three favorite animals are very fascinating creatures.

General Checklist: Check the Finished Paragraph	The Three-Point Expository Paragraph Outline
(1) Have you followed the pattern for a 3-point paragraph? (*Indent, topic sentence, 3-point sentence, 3 main points, 3 supporting sentences, and a concluding sentence.*) (2) Do you have complete sentences? (3) Have you capitalized the first word and put an end mark at the end of every sentence? (4) Have you checked your sentences for capitalization and punctuation mistakes? (5) Have you checked for misspelled words and incorrect homonym choices? (6) Have you indented each paragraph?	Topic 3 points about the topic Sentence #1: **Topic** sentence Sentence #2: A **three-point** sentence Sentence #3: A **first-point** sentence Sentence #4: A **supporting** sentence for the 1st point Sentence #5: A **second-point** sentence Sentence #6: A **supporting** sentence for the 2nd point Sentence #7: A **third-point** sentence Sentence #8: A **supporting** sentence for the 3rd point Sentence #9: A **concluding** sentence

Reference 31: Contraction Chart

Column 1		Column 2		Column 3	
Words Contracted	Contraction	Words Contracted	Contraction	Pronoun	Contraction
AM		**HAS**			
I am	I'm	has not	hasn't	**its**	**it's**
		he has	he's	(owns)	(it is)
IS		she has	she's	*its coat*	*it's cute*
is not	isn't				
he is	he's	**HAVE**			
she is	she's	have not	haven't	**your**	**you're**
it is	it's	I have	I've	(owns)	(you are)
who is	who's	you have	you've	*your car*	*you're right*
that is	that's	we have	we've		
what is	what's	they have	they've		
there is	there's			**their**	**they're**
		HAD		(owns)	(they are)
ARE		had not	hadn't	*their house*	*they're gone*
are not	aren't	I had	I'd		
you are	you're	he had	he'd		
we are	we're	she had	she'd	**whose**	**who's**
they are	they're	you had	you'd	(owns)	(who is)
		we had	we'd	*whose cat*	*who's going*
WAS, WERE		they had	they'd		
was not	wasn't				
were not	weren't	**WILL, SHALL**			
		will not	won't		
DO, DOES, DID		I will	I'll		
do not	don't	he will	he'll		
does not	doesn't	she will	she'll		
did not	didn't	you will	you'll		
		we will	we'll		
CAN		they will	they'll		
cannot	can't				
		WOULD			
LET		would not	wouldn't		
let us	let's	I would	I'd		
		he would	he'd		
		she would	she'd		
		you would	you'd		
		we would	we'd		
		they would	they'd		
		SHOULD, COULD			
		should not	shouldn't		
		could not	couldn't		

Sentence Samples:
1. (**Their**, They're) house is new.
2. We <u>have not</u> eaten today. **haven't**
3. He <u>doesn't</u> fish often. **does not**

Reference 32: Complete Sentences and Sentence Fragments

Identifying simple sentences and fragments: Write **S** for a complete sentence and **F** for a sentence fragment on the line beside each group of words below.

   S   1. Two monkeys wrestled playfully.

   F   2. Over the bridge.

   S   3. Taxi waited.

   S   4. Peter walks to the park.

   F   5. Ran around the fence.

   F   6. The tiny tadpoles.

Reference 33: Matching Subject Parts and Predicate Parts

Directions: Match each subject part with the correct predicate part by writing the correct sentence number in the blank.

Subject Parts		Predicate Parts
1. The tiny egg	**3**	stopped at the red light.
2. The hungry hawk	**2**	searched for food.
3. The yellow bus	**5**	melted on the bread.
4. The farmer	**1**	cracked slowly open.
5. The butter	**4**	harvested the wheat.

Reference 34: Correcting Sentence Fragments

Directions: Make each fragment below into a complete sentence. Underline the parts that are added.

1. Add a subject part to this fragment: **floated under the bridge**

   <u>**The wooden raft**</u> **floated under the bridge.**

2. Add a predicate part to this fragment: **The birds**

   The birds <u>**flew around the cage**</u>**.**

Level 2—Shurley English—Homeschool Edition

Reference 35: Descriptive Writing Guidelines

1. **When describing people,** it is helpful to notice these types of details:
   How they look, how they walk, how they talk, their way of doing things, any special event that happened to the person being described, and any other details that will help make that person stand out in your mind.

2. **When describing places or things,** it is helpful to notice these types of details:
   What you can see, smell, or touch (*including color, shape, size, age*), any other unusual information about a place or thing, any special event that happened in the place or to the thing being described, and whether or not the place or the thing is special to you.

3. **When describing nature,** it is helpful to notice these types of details:
   The special part or quality of the season, the sights, smells, sounds, colors, animals, insects, birds, and any special happening related to the scene being described.

4. **When describing an incident or an event,** it is helpful to notice these types of details:
   The order in which the events take place, any specific facts that will keep the story moving from a beginning to an ending, the answers to any of the *who, what, when, where, why,* and *how* questions that the reader needs to know, and especially the details that will create a clear picture, such as how things look, sound, smell, feel, etc.

Reference 36: Descriptive Paragraph Example

A. Sentence 1 is the topic sentence that introduces **what is being described.**
B. For Sentences 2-6, use **the descriptive details** in Reference 35.
C. Sentence 7 is a concluding sentence that **restates or relates back to the topic sentence.**

Thanksgiving Dinner

Every year, our family meets at Grandmother's house for a huge Thanksgiving feast. When we arrive, Grandmother is baking a delicious turkey in the oven. Aunt Carol brings a pumpkin pie, and Aunt Judy makes the dinner rolls. The kitchen fills with wonderful smells as dinner is being prepared. I quickly help Mom set the dinner table, and everyone gathers for a prayer of thanks. We sit down and enjoy our dinner and the time that we spend together. There is nothing like a Thanksgiving dinner at Grandmother's house.

Reference 37: Present, Past, and Future Verb Tenses

When you are writing paragraphs, you must use verbs that are in the same tense. Tense means time. The tense of a verb shows the time of the action. There are three basic tenses that show when an action takes place. They are **present tense, past tense,** and **future tense.** Now you will learn to recognize each kind of tense.

1. The **present tense** shows that something is happening now, in the present. Present tense verbs that are singular end in "s." Present tense verbs that are plural do not end in "s."

    (Singular present tense verb: walks) (Plural present tense verb: walk)
    (**Examples:** The girl walks to school. The girls walk to school.)

2. The **past tense** shows that something has happened sometime in the past. Most past tense verbs end in -ed, -d, or -t for both the singular and plural forms.

    (Singular past tense verb: walked) (Plural past tense verb: walked)
    (**Examples:** The girl walked to school. The girls walked to school.)

3. The **future tense** shows that something will happen sometime in the future. The future tense form has the helping verb *will* or *shall* before the main verb for both the singular and plural forms.

    (Singular future tense verb: will walk) (Plural future tense verb: will walk)
    (**Examples:** The girl will walk to school. The girls will walk to school.)

Present Tense	Past Tense	Future Tense
What to look for: **one verb** with s, es, or plain ending.	What to look for: **one verb** with -ed, -d, or -t.	What to look for: **will** or **shall** with a main verb.
The pirates search for the treasure.	The pirates searched for the treasure.	The pirates will search for the treasure.

Directions: Identify the tense of each underlined verb by writing a number **1** for present tense, a number **2** for past tense, and a number **3** for future tense.

Verb Tense	Verbs	Verb Tense	Verbs
2	1. They worked on the science project.	3	4. The snowflakes will drift to the ground.
3	2. They will work on the science project.	1	5. The snowflakes drift to the ground.
1	3. They work on the science project.	2	6. The snowflakes drifted to the ground.

Reference 38: Regular and Irregular Verbs

All verbs can be changed to past tense. The way you change a verb to past tense will make it a regular or irregular verb.

Regular Verbs: As you have just learned, you add -ed, -d, or -t to most verbs to form the past tense. Verbs that are made past tense by adding -ed, -d, or -t are called **regular verbs**. Most verbs are regular verbs because they form their past tense by adding -ed, -d, or -t.

Irregular Verbs: However, a few verbs, like the verbs on the irregular verb chart, are made past tense by a spelling change. The verbs from the verb chart are called **irregular verbs**. The only way to learn how to write and speak using irregular verbs is to memorize them.

1. **Regular and irregular present tense verbs:**
   (Regular present tense verbs: walk, walks) (Irregular present tense verbs: fall, falls)
   (**Examples:** The girls <u>walk</u> to school. The leaves <u>fall</u> from the tree.)

2. **Regular and irregular past tense verbs:**
   (Regular past tense verb: walked) (Irregular past tense verb: fell)
   (**Examples:** The girls <u>walked</u> to school. The leaves <u>fell</u> from the tree.)

3. **Regular and irregular future tense verbs:**
   (Regular future tense verb: will walk) (Irregular future tense verb: will fall)
   (**Examples:** The girls <u>will walk</u> to school. The leaves <u>will fall</u> from the tree.)

Present Tense	Past Tense	Future Tense
What to look for: **one verb** with s, es, or plain ending.	What to look for: **one verb** with -ed, -d, -t or an irregular spelling word.	What to look for: **will** or **shall** with a main verb.
1. We <u>climb</u> up the tree. 2. The ducks <u>fly</u> over the pond.	3. We <u>climbed</u> up the tree. 4. The ducks <u>flew</u> over the pond.	5. We <u>will climb</u> up the tree. 6. The ducks <u>will fly</u> over the pond.

Directions: Identify the tense of each underlined verb by writing a number **1** for present tense, a number **2** for past tense, or a number **3** for future tense. Use the verb chart for the irregular verbs.

Verb Tense	Regular Verbs	Verb Tense	Irregular Verbs
1	1. Grandmother <u>bakes</u> cookies.	1	4. We <u>drink</u> milk for breakfast.
2	2. Grandmother <u>baked</u> cookies.	2	5. We <u>drank</u> milk for breakfast.
3	3. Grandmother <u>will bake</u> cookies.	3	6. We <u>will drink</u> milk for breakfast.

Reference 39: Irregular Verb Chart

PRESENT	PAST	PAST PARTICIPLE		PRESENT PARTICIPLE	
become	became	(has)	become	(is)	becoming
blow	blew	(has)	blown	(is)	blowing
break	broke	(has)	broken	(is)	breaking
bring	brought	(has)	brought	(is)	bringing
burst	burst	(has)	burst	(is)	bursting
buy	bought	(has)	bought	(is)	buying
choose	chose	(has)	chosen	(is)	choosing
come	came	(has)	come	(is)	coming
drink	drank	(has)	drunk	(is)	drinking
drive	drove	(has)	driven	(is)	driving
eat	ate	(has)	eaten	(is)	eating
fall	fell	(has)	fallen	(is)	falling
fly	flew	(has)	flown	(is)	flying
freeze	froze	(has)	frozen	(is)	freezing
get	got	(has)	gotten	(is)	getting
give	gave	(has)	given	(is)	giving
grow	grew	(has)	grown	(is)	growing
know	knew	(has)	known	(is)	knowing
lie	lay	(has)	lain	(is)	lying
lay	laid	(has)	laid	(is)	laying
make	made	(has)	made	(is)	making
ride	rode	(has)	ridden	(is)	riding
ring	rang	(has)	rung	(is)	ringing
rise	rose	(has)	risen	(is)	rising
sell	sold	(has)	sold	(is)	selling
sing	sang	(has)	sung	(is)	singing
sink	sank	(has)	sunk	(is)	sinking
set	set	(has)	set	(is)	setting
sit	sat	(has)	sat	(is)	sitting
shoot	shot	(has)	shot	(is)	shooting
swim	swam	(has)	swum	(is)	swimming
take	took	(has)	taken	(is)	taking
tell	told	(has)	told	(is)	telling
throw	threw	(has)	thrown	(is)	throwing
wear	wore	(has)	worn	(is)	wearing
write	wrote	(has)	written	(is)	writing

Reference 40: Story Elements Outline

1. **Main Idea** (Tell the problem or situation that needs a solution.)
   Tracy is having a bad day.
2. **Setting** (Tell when and where the story takes place, either clearly stated or implied.)
   When – The story takes place on a rainy Friday afternoon.
   Where – The story takes place on Tracy's way home from school.
3. **Character** (Tell who or what the story is about.)
   The main characters are Tracy and her mom.
4. **Plot** (Tell what the characters in the story do and what happens to them.)
   The story is about Tracy's bad day.
5. **Ending** (Use a strong ending that will bring the story to a close.)
   The story ends with Tracy's mom leaving work early and surprising Tracy with homemade chocolate chip cookies.

Tracy's Gloomy Day

Tracy left school Friday with a sad look on her face. She pulled on her raincoat and sighed as she made her way home. The dark sky seemed to match her gloomy mood. As she walked a few blocks toward her house, she thought about all the horrible things that had happened that day. First of all, she was late to class. Then, she had to play by herself during recess because Laura, her best friend, was absent. Next, she forgot her lunch, and the cafeteria was serving chicken livers and Brussels sprouts. Suddenly, her stomach growled loudly.

When she was a block away from her house, it began to rain. She pulled the hood of her raincoat over her head and quickened her pace. She got to her house only to realize she had forgotten her key! She sat on the steps and began to cry. Just then, her mom opened the door. Tracy's mom had left work early and had prepared homemade chocolate chip cookies for Tracy. Tracy smiled as her mom helped her dry off. Now, Tracy's gloomy day had a wonderful ending as she followed her mother into the kitchen to eat warm, gooey cookies.

Reference 41: Tips for Writing Friendly Letters

Tip #1: Write as if you were talking to the person face-to-face. Share information about yourself and mutual friends. Tell stories, conversations, or jokes. Share photographs, articles, drawings, poems, etc. Avoid saying something about someone else that you'll be sorry for later.

Tip #2: If you are writing a return letter, be sure to answer any questions that were asked. Repeat the question so that your reader will know what you are writing about. (You asked about. . .)

Tip #3: End your letter in a positive way so that your reader will want to write a return letter.

Reference 42: Friendly Letter Sample

1. Heading
Write your address.
Write the date.

> 19 Colt Drive
> Rapid City, SD 29033
> April 12, 20____

2. Friendly Greeting, (or Salutation)
Name the person receiving the letter.
Use a comma.

> Dear Wesley,

3. Body (Indent Paragraphs)
Write what you want to say. Indent.

> Mom and Dad have decided to take our family vacation in Florida this year. Disney World will be so much fun! I hope you have a great summer break, too!

4. Closing,
Capitalize the first word.
Use a comma.

> Your cousin,

5. Signature
Sign your name.

> Sally

Reference 43: The Five Parts of a Friendly Letter

1. Heading
1. Box or street address of writer
2. City, state, zip code of writer
3. Date letter was written
4. Placement: upper right-hand corner

2. Friendly Greeting or Salutation
1. Begins with *Dear*
2. Names person receiving the letter
3. Has comma after person's name
4. Placement: at left margin, two lines below heading

3. Body
1. Tells reason the letter was written
2. Can have one or more paragraphs
3. Has indented paragraphs
4. Is placed one line after the greeting
5. Skips one line between each paragraph

4. Closing
1. Closes letter with a personal phrase-(Your friend, With love,)
2. Capitalizes only first word
3. Is followed by a comma
4. Is placed two lines below the body
5. Begins just to the right of the middle of the letter

5. Signature
1. Tells who wrote the letter
2. Is usually signed in cursive
3. Uses first name only unless there is a question as to which friend or relative you are
4. Is placed beneath the closing

Level 2—Shurley English—Homeschool Edition

Reference 44: Envelope Parts	**Friendly Envelope Sample**
The return address: 1. Name of the person writing the letter 2. Box or street address of the writer 3. City, state, zip code of the writer **The mailing address:** 1. Name of the person receiving the letter 2. Street address of the person receiving the letter 3. City, state, zip code of the person receiving the letter	**Return Address** — Write your name and address. **Stamp** Wesley Adams 19 Colt Drive Rapid City, SD 29033 **Mailing Address** — Write the name & address of the person receiving the letter. Sally Adams 89 West Brook Lane Blue Lake, NV 92800

Reference 45: Thank-You Note for a Gift

                                     For a Gift

What - Thank you for...
             (tell color, kind, and item)

Use - Tell how the gift is used.

Thanks - I appreciate your thinking of me at this time.

Example 1: Gift

Heading
87 West Brook Street
Billings, MT 11600
April 3, 20___

Greeting
Dear Matthew,

Body

    Thank you for the golden locket that you gave me for my birthday. It is very beautiful, and I wear it every day. Again, I thank you for the birthday gift.

Closing
Your friend,

Signature
Mary

Reference 46: Thank-You Note for an Action

<u>**For an Action**</u>

What - Thank you for...
(tell action)

Use - Tell how the action helped.

Thanks - I appreciate your remembering me.

Example 2: Action

Heading
251 Rose Court
Hempstead, NY 34800
September 16, 20___

Greeting
Dear Uncle John,

Body

 Thank you for taking me fishing on Saturday. Although we didn't catch much, I still had fun. I appreciate your spending time with me.

Closing
Your nephew,

Signature
David

Reference 47: Three Main Parts of the Library

Fiction Section
Fiction books contain stories about people, places, or things that are not true.

Nonfiction Section
Nonfiction books contain information and stories that are true.

Reference Section
The Reference Section is designed to help you find information on many topics. The most common reference books are the dictionary and the encyclopedia.

Level 2—Shurley English—Homeschool Edition

Reference 48: The Front Parts of a Book

AT THE FRONT:

1. **Title Page.** This page has the full title of the book, the author's name, the illustrator's name, the name of the publishing company, and the city where the book was published.

2. **Copyright Page.** This page is right after the title page and tells the year in which the book was published and who owns the copyright. If the book has an ISBN number (International Standard Book Number), it is listed here.

3. **Preface** (also called **introduction**). If a book has this page, it will come before the table of contents and will usually tell briefly why the book was written and what it is about.

4. **Table of Contents.** This section lists the major divisions of the book by units or chapters and tells their page numbers.

5. **Body.** This is the main section, or text, of the book.

Reference 49: The Back Parts of a Book

AT THE BACK:

1. **Appendix.** This section includes extra informative material such as maps, charts, tables, diagrams, letters, etc. It is always wise to find out what is in the appendix, since it may contain supplementary material that you could otherwise find only by going to the library.

2. **Glossary.** This section is like a dictionary and gives the meanings of some of the important words in the book.

3. **Bibliography.** This section includes a list of books used by the author. It could serve as a guide for further reading on a topic.

4. **Index.** This will probably be your most useful section. The purpose of the index is to help you quickly locate information about the topics in the book. It has an alphabetical list of specific topics and tells on which page that information can be found. It is similar to the table of contents, but it is much more detailed.

PRACTICE

SECTION

Chapter 1, Lesson 3, Practice: Put each group of words in alphabetical order. Write numbers in the blanks to show the order in each column.

Travel Words	Picnic Words	"D" Words	Family Words
_____ 1. airport	_____ 5. sandwich	_____ 9. dolphin	_____ 13. mother
_____ 2. luggage	_____ 6. blanket	_____ 10. dog	_____ 14. father
_____ 3. ticket	_____ 7. basket	_____ 11. daisy	_____ 15. brother
_____ 4. hotel	_____ 8. ants	_____ 12. dragon	_____ 16. sister

Chapter 2, Lesson 4, Practice 1: Put each group of words in alphabetical order. Use numbers 1-4 in the blanks to show the order in each column.

Restaurant Words	"A" Words
_____ 1. menu	_____ 5. apple
_____ 2. chef	_____ 6. alligator
_____ 3. table	_____ 7. afternoon
_____ 4. waiter	_____ 8. album

Chapter 2, Lesson 4, Practice 2: Put the letters below in alphabetical order.

o s i b j p z d _____

Chapter 2, Lesson 4, Practice 3: Match the definitions. Write the correct letter beside each numbered concept.

_____	1. verb question	A.	what
_____	2. subject-noun question (thing)	B.	a capital letter
_____	3. parts of a complete sentence	C.	verb
_____	4. noun	D.	person, place, or thing
_____	5. subject-noun question (person)	E.	sentence
_____	6. sentences should begin with	F.	subject, verb, complete sense
_____	7. tells what the subject does	G.	who
_____	8. ends with an end mark	H.	what is being said about

Level 2—Shurley English—Homeschool Edition

Chapter 3, Lesson 2, Practice: Write *a* or *an* in the blanks.

1. The car had ___ alarm.	4. Joe caught ___ cricket.	7. ___ owner	10. ___ whisker
2. The ship dodged ___ iceberg.	5. My truck has ___ oil leak.	8. ___ guitar	11. ___ author
3. Stacy baked ___ pecan pie.	6. Amanda chased ___ rabbit.	9. ___ injury	12. ___ balloon

Chapter 3, Lesson 3, Practice 1: Match the definitions. Write the correct letter beside each numbered concept.

_____	1. sentences should begin with	A.	verb
_____	2. adjective modifies	B.	capital letter
_____	3. verb question	C.	noun or pronoun
_____	4. tells what the subject does	D.	person, place, or thing
_____	5. subject-noun question (thing)	E.	who
_____	6. parts of a complete sentence	F.	subject, verb, complete sense
_____	7. noun	G.	what
_____	8. subject-noun question (person)	H.	what is being said about
_____	9. adverb modifies	I.	verb, adjective, or adverb

Chapter 3, Lesson 3, Practice 2: Write *a* or *an* in the blanks.

1. Alex took ___ bath.	4. I ate ___ cup of yogurt.	7. ___ boat	10. ___ cloud
2. Sue bought ___ outfit.	5. Fred visited ___ old museum.	8. ___ freckle	11. ___ insect
3. Mother picked ___ iris.	6. Laura has ___ headache.	9. ___ owl	12. ___ eagle

Chapter 3, Lesson 4, Practice 1: Name the four parts of speech that you have studied. (*You may use abbreviations.*)

1. _____   2. _____   3. _____   4. _____

Chapter 3, Lesson 4, Practice 2: Match the definitions. Write the correct letter beside each numbered concept.

_____	1. sentences should begin with	A.	noun or pronoun
_____	2. adjective modifies	B.	verb
_____	3. verb question	C.	capital letter
_____	4. tells what the subject does	D.	person, place, or thing
_____	5. subject-noun question (thing)	E.	what is being said about
_____	6. parts of a complete sentence	F.	verb, adjective, or adverb
_____	7. noun	G.	what
_____	8. subject-noun question (person)	H.	subject, verb, complete sense
_____	9. adverb modifies	I.	who

Chapter 3, Lesson 4, Practice 3: Write *a* or *an* in the blanks.

1. Henry was _____ poet.   4. He caught _____ fish.   7. _____ house   10. _____ pickle
2. Beth found _____ acorn.   5. She ate _____ olive.   8. _____ diamond   11. _____ almond
3. They lived in _____ igloo.   6. We carved _____ pumpkin.   9. _____ eyelash   12. _____ ocean

---

Chapter 4, Lesson 2, Practice 1: Put the end mark and the abbreviation for each kind of sentence in the blanks below.

1. Did you see the game last night   _____

2. That huge tree branch fell on my new car   _____

3. Stephanie ate a hamburger for lunch   _____

Level 2—Shurley English—Homeschool Edition

Chapter 4, Lesson 2, Practice 2: Match the definitions. Write the correct letter beside each numbered concept.

_____	1. expresses strong feeling	A.	exclamatory sentence
_____	2. makes a statement	B.	interrogative sentence
_____	3. adjective modifies	C.	noun or pronoun
_____	4. article adjectives can be called	D.	verb, adjective, or adverb
_____	5. subject question	E.	who or what
_____	6. asks a question	F.	person, place, or thing
_____	7. noun	G.	verb
_____	8. tells what the subject does	H.	noun markers
_____	9. adverb modifies	I.	declarative sentence

Chapter 4, Lesson 2, Practice 3

On notebook paper, write a sentence to demonstrate each of these three kinds of sentences: (1) Declarative, (2) Interrogative, and (3) Exclamatory. Write the correct punctuation and the abbreviation that identifies it at the end. Use these abbreviations: **D, Int, E.**

Chapter 4, Lesson 3, Practice 1: Put the end mark and the abbreviation for each kind of sentence in the blanks below.

1. My green marker fell on the floor _____

2. How old is your brother _____

3. I spilled grape juice on my best suit _____

Chapter 4, Lesson 3, Practice 2: Match the definitions. Write the correct letter beside each numbered concept.

_____	1. sentences should begin with	A.	noun marker
_____	2. article adjectives	B.	a, an, the
_____	3. adjective modifies	C.	what
_____	4. verb question	D.	a capital letter
_____	5. tells what the subject does	E.	verb
_____	6. subject-noun question (thing)	F.	what is being said about
_____	7. article adjective can be called	G.	person, place, or thing
_____	8. parts of a complete sentence	H.	verb, adjective, or adverb
_____	9. noun	I.	subject, verb, complete sense
_____	10. subject-noun question (person)	J.	noun or pronoun
_____	11. adverb modifies	K.	who

Chapter 4, Lesson 3, Practice 3: Write *a* or *an* in the blanks.

1. Kate read ___ magazine.   3. He built ___ tree house.   5. ___ orphan   7. ___ picture
2. We found ___ empty bottle. 4. Joe saw ___ raccoon.   6. ___ umbrella   8. ___ oatmeal pie

---

Chapter 4, Lesson 3, Practice 4: Name the four parts of speech that you have studied. (*You may use abbreviations.*)

1. _____   2. _____   3. _____   4. _____

Chapter 5, Lesson 1, Practice 1: For each noun listed below, write **S** for singular or **P** for plural.

Noun	S or P	Noun	S or P	Noun	S or P
1. cake		4. soup		7. shells	
2. telephones		5. flags		8. grass	
3. mice		6. street		9. buttons	

Level 2—Shurley English—Homeschool Edition

Chapter 5, Lesson 1, Practice 2: Write *a* or *an* in the blanks.

1. We stayed at ___ hotel. 3. The waiter dropped ___ spoon. 5. ___ boulder 7. ___ eraser
2. That is just ___ excuse. 4. They live in ___ country cottage. 6. ___ agency 8. ___ object

Chapter 5, Lesson 1, Practice 3: Put the end mark and the abbreviation for each kind of sentence in the blanks below.

1. William moved to Vermont _____

2. Is it dark outside _____

3. The wind just blew our candle out _____

Chapter 5, Lesson 1, Practice 4: Name the four parts of speech that you have studied. (*You may use abbreviations.*)

1. _____ 2. _____ 3. _____ 4. _____

Chapter 5, Lesson 2, Practice 1: For each noun listed below, write **C** for common or **P** for proper.

Noun	C or P	Noun	C or P	Noun	C or P
1. book		4. April		7. Thanksgiving	
2. Italian		5. Tuesday		8. tractor	
3. sock		6. month		9. holiday	

Chapter 5, Lesson 2, Practice 2: For each noun listed below, write **S** for singular or **P** for plural.

Noun	S or P	Noun	S or P	Noun	S or P
1. mountain		4. olive		7. nose	
2. parks		5. caves		8. spoons	
3. statues		6. hole		9. stripes	

Chapter 5, Lesson 2, Practice 3: Write *a* or *an* in the blanks.

1. They are building _____ bank.   3. Dad built _____ fire.   5. _____ bag   7. _____ acre
2. He drives _____ orange truck.   4. We had _____ pop quiz.   6. _____ index   8. _____ flake

---

Chapter 5, Lesson 2, Practice 4: Name the four parts of speech that you have studied. (*You may use abbreviations.*)

1. _____   2. _____   3. _____   4. _____

Chapter 5, Lesson 5, Practice 1: Finding the topic: Write the name of the topic that best describes what each row of words is about. Choose from these topics:

Colors	Sweets	Animals	Seasons	Kitchen Things	Holidays

(1)	(2)	(3)
_____	_____	_____
Easter	cake	spoon
Christmas	cookies	bowl
Labor Day	ice cream	pan
Thanksgiving	pie	oven

Chapter 5, Lesson 5, Practice 2: Words that support the topic: In each row, cross out the one idea that does not support the underlined topic at the top.

(1)	(2)	(3)
Farm Animals	Pets	Vegetables
horse	dog	green bean
shoe	cat	squash
cow	goldfish	valley
pig	peach	potato
chicken	parrot	okra

Level 2—Shurley English—Homeschool Edition

Chapter 5, Lesson 5, Practice 3: Sentences that support the topic: Read each topic. Then, cross out the one sentence that does not support the topic.

Topic: A Marvelous Fairy Tale

1. The prince saves the princess.
2. The prince lives in a large castle.
3. My sister loves to read fairy tales.
4. The prince and princess live happily ever after.

Topic: Signs of Spring

1. The grass in the yard turns green.
2. Spring and summer are my favorite seasons.
3. The weather turns warmer.
4. Flowers begin to bloom.

Chapter 6, Lesson 1, Practice 1: Underline the complete subject once and the complete predicate twice.

1. Several little puppies played happily.
2. The old bus stopped suddenly.
3. A giant toad hopped away.
4. The tiny tadpoles darted quickly around.

Chapter 6, Lesson 1, Practice 2: Underline the simple subject once and the simple predicate twice.

1. A baby robin chirped loudly.
2. The two toddlers played tirelessly.
3. The black kettle fell.
4. The new student sat quietly.

Chapter 6, Lesson 2, Practice 1: Classify the sentence below. Underline the complete subject once and the complete predicate twice. Then, complete the table below.

The   Christmas   ornaments   sparkled   brightly.

List the Noun Used	List the Noun Job	Singular or Plural	Common or Proper	Simple Subject	Simple Predicate

Page 42 - Practice Section

Chapter 6, Lesson 2, Practice 2: Underline the complete subject once and the complete predicate twice.

1. The new toy broke suddenly.
2. The office staff laughed loudly.
3. A wildfire burned brightly ahead.
4. The jet airliner flew away.

Chapter 6, Lesson 2, Practice 3: Underline the simple subject once and the simple predicate twice.

1. An empty bottle broke.
2. The three red tulips bloomed.
3. The tomatoes ripened quickly.
4. Many horses trot contentedly.

Chapter 6, Lesson 2, Practice 4: For each noun listed below, write **C** for common or **P** for proper.

Noun	C or P	Noun	C or P	Noun	C or P
1. jacket		3. month		5. pizza	
2. Phillip		4. insect		6. October	

Chapter 6, Lesson 2, Practice 5: For each noun listed below, write **S** for singular or **P** for plural.

Noun	S or P	Noun	S or P	Noun	S or P
1. plants		3. tractors		5. socks	
2. mop		4. glass		6. lions	

Chapter 6, Lesson 5, Practice 1: Finding the topic: Write the name of the topic that best describes what each row of words is about. Choose from these topics:

Colors **Food** **Animals** **Seasons** **Kitchen Things** **Transportation**

(1)	(2)	(3)
pizza	motorcycle	pan
taco	car	refrigerator
hamburger	scooter	sink
burrito	truck	knife

Chapter 6, Lesson 5, Practice 2: Words that support the topic: In each row, cross out the one idea that does not support the underlined topic at the top.

(1) Zoo Animals	(2) Shapes	(3) Colors
tiger	oval	red
clown	rectangle	green
ostrich	square	valley
ape	pepperoni	brown
tortoise	circle	pink

Chapter 6, Lesson 5, Practice 3: Sentences that support the topic: Read each topic. Then, cross out the one sentence that does not support the topic.

Topic: A Trip to the Circus

1. Dad took me to the circus yesterday.
2. Dad gave our tickets to the lady in the booth.
3. My dad took me to the movies last week.
4. We found our seats and waited patiently for the show to begin.

Topic: An Exciting New Game Show

1. The contestants stand nervously in front of the cameras.
2. My uncle is a newscaster on channel eight.
3. The host asks each player a different question.
4. The player with the highest score wins a new car.

Chapter 7, Lesson 1, Practice: Classify the sentence below. Underline the complete subject once and the complete predicate twice. Then, complete the table below.

_____ The   large   helium   balloon   floated   freely.

List the Noun Used	List the Noun Job	Singular or Plural	Common or Proper	Simple Subject	Simple Predicate

Chapter 7, Lesson 5, Practice Writing Page: Use the two-point outline form below to guide you as you write a two-point expository paragraph.

Write a topic: _____

List 2 points about the topic:

1. _____ 2. _____

Sentence #1	Topic sentence (*Use words in the topic and tell how many points will be used.*)
Sentence #2	2-point sentence (*List your 2 points in the order that you will present them.*)
Sentence #3	State your first point in a complete sentence.
Sentence #4	Write a supporting sentence for the first point.
Sentence #5	State your second point in a complete sentence.
Sentence #6	Write a supporting sentence for the second point.
Sentence #7	Concluding sentence (*Restate the topic sentence and add an extra thought.*)

Student Note: Rewrite your seven-sentence paragraph on notebook paper. Be sure to indent and use the checklists to help you edit your paragraph. Make sure you re-read your paragraph slowly several times.

Chapter 9, Lesson 1, Practice: Underline the correct homonym in each sentence.

1. He (threw, through) the ball to Alex.
2. I want to travel (to, too, two) Alaska.
3. Jeremy walked (threw, through) the front door.
4. Shelly had (to, too, two) new dresses.
5. The ship sank (to, too, two) quickly.
6. You need to stand in line over (hear, here).
7. Mom (sent, scent) me to the store.
8. I didn't (hear, here) the alarm clock.

Chapter 9, Lesson 2, Practice: Underline the correct homonym in each sentence.

1. The (led, lead) pipes were replaced.
2. These are my (knew, new) boots.
3. She (led, lead) me to my classroom.
4. My dad (knew, new) your grandfather.
5. The church (council, counsel) cast the final vote.
6. The doctor gave (council, counsel) to his patients.
7. There are seven (days, daze) in a week.
8. The excitement left me in a (days, daze).

Chapter 9, Lesson 3, Practice: Underline the correct homonym in each sentence.

1. Is this (your, you're) book?
2. The group went (to, too, two) the mall.
3. I need some (peace, piece) and quiet.
4. (Your, You're) Katie's partner.
5. She ate another (peace, piece) of pizza.
6. We placed (forth, fourth) in the tournament.
7. They were gone for an entire (week, weak).
8. My knees felt (weak, week) during the recital.

Chapter 10, Lesson 1, Practice 1: For each sentence, do these four things: (1) Write the subject. (2) Write **S** if the subject is singular or **P** if the subject is plural. (3) Write the rule number. (4) Underline the correct verb in the sentence.

Rule 1: A singular subject must use a singular verb form that ends in **s**: *is, was, has, does,* or *verbs ending with* **es**.

Rule 2: A plural subject, a compound subject, or the subject **YOU** must use a plural verb form that has **no s** ending: *are, were, do, have, or verbs without* **s** *or* **es** *endings.* (A plural verb form is also called the *plain form.*)

Subject	S or P	Rule

1. The penguins (shuffles, shuffle) across the ice.
2. The lemonade and tea (is, are) in the refrigerator.
3. Tyler's boat (glides, glide) across the lake.
4. Larry (play, plays) in the sandbox.
5. You (washes, wash) your hands.
6. Her stomach (growls, growl) loudly.
7. The curtains (flutter, flutters) in the breeze.
8. The chefs (prepares, prepare) the dinner.
9. Tom and Jennifer (takes, take) the dog on a walk.
10. Several women (quilt, quilts) happily.

Chapter 10, Lesson 1, Practice 2: Underline the correct homonym in each sentence.

1. She said to turn (right, write).
2. I didn't (know, no) the answer.
3. The steel wool felt (course, coarse).
4. We ate a five (coarse, course) meal.
5. She will (write, right) on the board.
6. Peter answered (no, know) to her question.

Chapter 10, Lesson 2, Practice 1: For each sentence, do these four things: (1) Write the subject. (2) Write **S** if the subject is singular or **P** if the subject is plural. (3) Write the rule number. (4) Underline the correct verb in the sentence.

Rule 1: A singular subject must use a singular verb form that ends in **s**: *is, was, has, does, or verbs ending with* **es**.

Rule 2: A plural subject, a compound subject, or the subject **YOU** must use a plural verb form that has **no s** ending: *are, were, do, have, or verbs without* **s** *or* **es** *endings.* (A plural verb form is also called the *plain form*.)

Subject	S or P	Rule

1. The bugs (swarms, swarm) the chocolate cake.
2. Josh and Steven (plays, play) soccer.
3. The cloud (covers, cover) the bright sun.
4. My aunt (work, works) at a bank.
5. You (helps, help) gather the trash.
6. We (rakes, rake) the leaves into a pile.
7. The bus (stop, stops) at the railroad tracks.
8. The buckets (leaks, leak) onto the floor.
9. Tony (asks, ask) politely for permission.

Chapter 10, Lesson 2, Practice 2: Underline the correct homonym in each sentence.

1. Our school's (principal, principle) won the award.
2. We learned the basic (principles, principals).
3. Please direct your attention over (their, there).
4. The group visited the (capital, capitol) building.
5. Georgia's (capitol, capital) is Atlanta.
6. She showed us a (capital, capitol) letter.
7. I wanted to visit (their, there) new home.
8. Timothy ran (to, too, two) the bus stop.

Chapter 10, Lesson 3, Practice 1: Underline the correct homonym in each sentence.

1. Todd placed (fourth, forth) in the race.
2. We'll meet (here, hear) in one hour.
3. Jackie (knew, new) where to shop.
4. Patsy (lead, led) me to the door.
5. The lion jumped (threw, through) the hoops.
6. The nation's (piece, peace) was not long-lasting.
7. The mayor appointed Jim to the (counsel, council).
8. There are only three (days, daze) until my birthday.

Chapter 10, Lesson 3, Practice 2: For each sentence, do these four things: (1) Write the subject. (2) Write **S** if the subject is singular or **P** if the subject is plural. (3) Write the rule number. (4) Underline the correct verb in the sentence.

Rule 1: A singular subject must use a singular verb form that ends in **s**: *is, was, has, does,* or verbs ending with **es**.

Rule 2: A plural subject, a compound subject, or the subject **YOU** must use a plural verb form that has **no s** ending: *are, were, do, have,* or verbs without **s** or **es** endings. (A plural verb form is also called the *plain form*.)

Subject	S or P	Rule

1. The pineapples (ripens, ripen) in the hot sun.
2. The squirrels (enjoys, enjoy) our bird bath.
3. My lunchbox (falls, fall) off the counter top.
4. The ship (dock, docks) quickly at the port.
5. You (needs, need) to drink more milk.
6. Her socks (clings, cling) tightly to her ankles.
7. The firemen (rush, rushes) quickly to the scene.
8. The helicopter (land, lands) safely on the pad.
9. The trumpets (plays, play) the melody.

Chapter 11, Lesson 1, Practice: For each sentence, do these four things: (1) Write the subject. (2) Write **S** if the subject is singular or **P** if the subject is plural. (3) Write the rule number. (4) Underline the correct verb in the sentence.

Rule 1: A singular subject must use a singular verb form that ends in **s**: *is, was, has, does,* or verbs ending with **es**.

Rule 2: A plural subject, a compound subject, or the subject **YOU** must use a plural verb form that has **no s** ending: *are, were, do, have,* or verbs without **s** or **es** endings. (A plural verb form is also called the *plain form*.)

Subject	S or P	Rule	
			1. The stars (shines, shine) brightly in the night sky.
			2. Peter and Jerry (lives, live) on the same street.
			3. We (visit, visits) the new theme park.
			4. Josh (think, thinks) about the questions on the test.
			5. The piano teacher (speak, speaks) quietly to the new student.
			6. The flowers (wilt, wilts) in the dry summer months.
			7. He (sends, send) the letter to the company.
			8. The cookies (sits, sit) on a plate in the kitchen.
			9. The triplets (plays, play) under the sprinkler.
			10. The scout (find, finds) the enemy base.
			11. The men (board, boards) the trolley car.
			12. Several gophers (tunnel, tunnels) underground.

Chapter 11, Lesson 2, Practice 1: Underline the correct homonym in each sentence.

1. Debbie has (to, too, two) sisters.
2. The desert is (to, too, two) hot.
3. She bought new (stationery, stationary).
4. (Their, There) meeting started at five.
5. The ball went (threw, through) the window.
6. May I come to (your, you're) birthday party.
7. I found the last (piece, peace) of the puzzle.
8. The train stood (stationery, stationary) yesterday.

Chapter 11, Lesson 2, Practice 2: For each sentence, do these four things: (1) Write the subject. (2) Write **S** if the subject is singular or **P** if the subject is plural. (3) Write the rule number. (4) Underline the correct verb in the sentence.

Rule 1: A singular subject must use a singular verb form that ends in **s**: *is, was, has, does,* or verbs ending with **es**.

Rule 2: A plural subject, a compound subject, or the subject **YOU** must use a plural verb form that has **no s** ending: *are, were, do, have,* or verbs without **s** or **es** *endings.* (A plural verb form is also called the *plain form.*)

Subject	S or P	Rule

1. My brother (climb, climbs) the big oak tree.
2. The woman's scarf (drape, drapes) around her neck.
3. The whales (move, moves) slowly through the ocean.
4. The light (flash, flashes) on top of the tower.
5. You (moves, move) your truck over there.
6. The ripened peaches (falls, fall) from the tree.
7. The vine (grow, grows) up the side of the building.
8. The voices (echoes, echo) in the tunnel.
9. Our campfire (burns, burn) brightly.

Chapter 11, Lesson 3, Practice 1: Underline the correct homonym in each sentence.

1. Try our (knew, new) milkshake.
2. That is the (right, write) answer.
3. I (knew, new) you could do it!
4. Place your hand (here, hear).
5. The girls ran (threw, through) the sprinkler.
6. The waiter (through, threw) down his apron.
7. Can you (hear, here) my heartbeat?
8. I should (write, right) a letter to the company.

Level 2—Shurley English—Homeschool Edition

Chapter 11, Lesson 3, Practice 2: For each sentence, do these four things: (1) Write the subject. (2) Write **S** if the subject is singular or **P** if the subject is plural. (3) Write the rule number. (4) Underline the correct verb in the sentence.

Rule 1: A singular subject must use a singular verb form that ends in **s**: *is, was, has, does, or verbs ending with* **es**.

Rule 2: A plural subject, a compound subject, or the subject **YOU** must use a plural verb form that has **no s** ending: *are, were, do, have, or verbs without* **s** *or* **es** *endings.* (A plural verb form is also called the *plain form.*)

Subject	S or P	Rule

1. The newscasters (reports, report) the forest fire.
2. The games (begins, begin) tomorrow.
3. Jill (searches, search) for her purse.
4. The wind (gust, gusts) across the plains.
5. You (turns, turn) left at the stoplight.
6. The conferences (was, were) held in the new arena.
7. The dew (covers, cover) the lawn.
8. Several bills quickly (passes, pass) through Congress.
9. The billboards (dots, dot) the highway.

Chapter 12, Lesson 2, Practice: Correct the capitalization mistakes and put the rule number above each correction. Use the rule numbers in Reference 24 on page 18 in the Reference Section of your book.

_____ (capitalization rule numbers)

1. jan has an appointment with dr. jones on tuesday.   (Editing Guide: 4 capitalization mistakes)

_____ (capitalization rule numbers)

2. i took a picture of aunt mary and uncle james.   (Editing Guide: 5 capitalization mistakes)

Chapter 12, Lesson 3, Practice 1: For each sentence, do these four things: (1) Write the subject. (2) Write **S** if the subject is singular or **P** if the subject is plural. (3) Write the rule number. (4) Underline the correct verb in the sentence.

Rule 1: A singular subject must use a singular verb form that ends in **s**: *is, was, has, does,* or verbs ending with **es**.

Rule 2: A plural subject, a compound subject, or the subject **YOU** must use a plural verb form that has **no s** ending: *are, were, do, have,* or verbs without **s** or **es** endings. (A plural verb form is also called the *plain form*.)

Subject	S or P	Rule

1. The mattress (sag, sags) when we sit on it.
2. The mud (dries, dry) on the edges of the pond.
3. The radishes (ripen, ripens) in the garden.
4. My taco (taste, tastes) good.
5. The stones (skips, skip) across the pond.

Chapter 12, Lesson 3, Practice 2: Underline the correct homonym in each sentence.

1. The cashier gave me a (new, knew) coin.
2. Can you (here, hear) the robin singing?
3. (No, Know), I don't need your help.
4. (There, They're) going to the movies.
5. A sentence begins with a (capital, capitol) letter.
6. Joey (threw, through) the baseball to Tom.

Chapter 12, Lesson 3, Practice 3: Correct the capitalization mistakes and put the rule number above each correction. Use the rule numbers in Reference 24 on page 18 in the Reference Section of your book.

_____ (capitalization rule numbers)

1. my uncle john and i like to hunt.   **(Editing Guide: 4 capitalization mistakes)**

_____ (capitalization rule numbers)

2. jared and sam are traveling to spain in may.   **(Editing Guide: 4 capitalization mistakes)**

Level 2—Shurley English—Homeschool Edition

Chapter 13, Lesson 2, Practice: Correct the capitalization and punctuation mistakes for sentences 1-3. Write the rule numbers above the capitalization corrections and below the punctuation corrections. Use Reference 24 for the capitalization rules and Reference 26 for the punctuation rules. The references are located on pages 18 and 19 in your Reference Section.

_____ (capitalization rule numbers)

1. sam and i were both born on january 19 1992   (Editing Guide: 3 capitals & 2 punctuation)

_____ (punctuation rule numbers)

_____ (capitalization rule numbers)

2. dr   murphy   has   a   clinic   in   dayton   ohio   (Editing Guide: 4 capitals & 3 punctuation)

_____ (punctuation rule numbers)

_____ (capitalization rule numbers)

3. chad and jeff rode their bikes down willow street   (Editing Guide: 4 capitals & 1 punctuation)

_____ (punctuation rule numbers)

Chapter 13, Lesson 3, Practice 1: Underline the correct homonym in each sentence.

1. I (no, know) how to fix the computer.
2. The cat didn't fit (through, threw) the hole.
3. She received a (fourth, forth) place ribbon.
4. Please raise your (write, right) hand.
5. Allen went (to, too, two) the beach.
6. (It's, Its) so good to see you!

Chapter 13, Lesson 3, Practice 2: Correct the capitalization and punctuation mistakes. Write the rule numbers above the capitalization corrections and below the punctuation corrections. Use Reference 24 for the capitalization rules and Reference 26 for the punctuation rules. The references are located on pages 18 and 19 in your Reference Section.

_____ (capitalization rule numbers)

1. chris   goes   to   school   in   oxford   mississippi   (Editing Guide: 3 capitals & 2 punctuation)

_____ (punctuation rule numbers)

_____ (capitalization rule numbers)

2. mr   thorton   has   a   birthday   on   thursday   (Editing Guide: 3 capitals & 2 punctuation)

_____ (punctuation rule numbers)

Chapter 14, Lesson 1, Practice 1: Underline the correct homonym in each sentence.

1. Mr. Wilson is a high school (principle, principal).
2. The crowd cheered when (their, there) team won.
3. The (week, weak) branch broke off the tree.
4. The water in the tub is (to, too, two) hot.
5. I used a (lead, led) pencil on the test.
6. I would like a (piece, peace) of candy.

Chapter 14, Lesson 1, Practice 2: Correct the capitalization and punctuation mistakes. Write the rule numbers above the capitalization corrections and below the punctuation corrections. Use Reference 24 for the capitalization rules and Reference 26 for the punctuation rules. The references are located on pages 18 and 19 in your Reference Section.

_____ (capitalization rule numbers)

1. julie started the beautiful quilt on april 2 2002   (Editing Guide: 2 capitals & 2 punctuation)

_____ (punctuation rule numbers)

_____ (capitalization rule numbers)

2. his team played in the arena at san antonio texas   (Editing Guide: 4 capitals & 2 punctuation)

_____ (punctuation rule numbers)

Chapter 14, Lesson 2, Practice 1: Underline the correct homonym in each sentence.

1. The runners said the (course, coarse) was difficult.
2. The company invented a (knew, new) product.
3. The (capitol, capital) building was built in 1876.
4. She (scent, sent) cookies to the party.
5. The clowns painted (their, there) faces.
6. I feel like I could sleep for (days, daze).

Chapter 14, Lesson 2, Practice 2: Correct the capitalization and punctuation mistakes. Write the rule numbers above the capitalization corrections and below the punctuation corrections. Use Reference 24 for the capitalization rules and Reference 26 for the punctuation rules. The references are located on pages 18 and 19 in your Reference Section.

_____ (capitalization rule numbers)

1. was j r r johnson from augusta maine   (Editing Guide: 7 capitals & 5 punctuation)

_____ (punctuation rule numbers)

Level 2—Shurley English—Homeschool Edition

Chapter 14, Lesson 2, Practice 3: For each sentence, do these four things: (1) Write the subject. (2) Write **S** if the subject is singular or **P** if the subject is plural. (3) Write the rule number. (4) Underline the correct verb in the sentence.

Rule 1: A singular subject must use a singular verb form that ends in **s**: *is, was, has, does,* or verbs ending with **es**.

Rule 2: A plural subject, a compound subject, or the subject **YOU** must use a plural verb form that has **no s** ending: *are, were, do, have,* or verbs without **s** or **es** endings. (A plural verb form is also called the *plain form*.)

Subject	S or P	Rule	
			1. The motorists cautiously (drive, drives) through the tunnel.
			2. Cows (grazes, graze) contentedly in the pasture.
			3. The apple cider (cools, cool) in my mug.
			4. The duckling (hatch, hatches) from the tiny egg.
			5. You (catches, catch) the ball.
			6. Several kites (flies, fly) above our heads.
			7. The tea kettle (whistles, whistle) in the kitchen.
			8. The circus clowns (carries, carry) balloons.

Chapter 14, Lesson 3, Practice 1: Underline the correct homonym in each sentence.

1. I couldn't (hear, here) the telephone ring.
2. We (threw, through) a surprise party for Joe.
3. The citizens prayed for (peace, piece).
4. The puppy searched for (it's, its) bone.

Chapter 14, Lesson 3, Practice 2: Correct the capitalization and punctuation mistakes. Write the rule numbers above the capitalization corrections and below the punctuation corrections. Use Reference 24 for the capitalization rules and Reference 26 for the punctuation rules. The references are located on pages 18 and 19 in your Reference Section.

_____ (capitalization rule numbers)

1. the letter was dated july 6 2001 (Editing Guide: 2 capitals & 2 punctuation)

_____ (punctuation rule numbers)

_____ (capitalization rule numbers)

2. dana and tiffany are my cousins from richmond virginia (Editing Guide: 4 capitals & 2 punctuation)

_____ (punctuation rule numbers)

Chapter 15, Lesson 1, Practice 1

On a sheet of paper, write seven subject pronouns and seven possessive pronouns.

Chapter 15, Lesson 1, Practice 2: For each sentence, do these four things: (1) Write the subject. (2) Write **S** if the subject is singular or **P** if the subject is plural. (3) Write the rule number. (4) Underline the correct verb in the sentence.

Rule 1: A singular subject must use a singular verb form that ends in **s**: *is, was, has, does, or verbs ending with es.*

Rule 2: A plural subject, a compound subject, or the subject **YOU** must use a plural verb form that has **no s** ending: *are, were, do, have, or verbs without* **s** *or* **es** *endings.* (A plural verb form is also called the *plain form.*)

Subject	S or P	Rule

1. The raindrops (splashes, splash) in the puddle.
2. The lazy cat (yawns, yawn) sleepily.
3. The singers (smiles, smile) at the audience.
4. The container of salt (spill, spills) on the floor.
5. You (cuts, cut) the page in half.

Chapter 15, Lesson 1, Practice 3: Underline the correct homonym in each sentence.

1. The child ignored his mother's (counsel, council).
2. (There, They're) helping at the banquet.
3. They brought (their, they're) own lunch.
4. The deli is located over (their, there).

Chapter 15, Lesson 1, Practice 4: Correct the capitalization and punctuation mistakes. Write the rule numbers above the capitalization corrections and below the punctuation corrections. Use Reference 24 for the capitalization rules and Reference 26 for the punctuation rules. The references are located on page 18 and 19 in your Reference Section.

_____ (capitalization rule numbers)

1. may i meet with dr lewis on tuesday   (Editing Guide: 5 capitals & 2 punctuation)

_____ (punctuation rule numbers)

Level 2—Shurley English—Homeschool Edition

Chapter 15, Lesson 2, Practice: First, identify each noun as singular or plural by writing **S** or **P** in the first blank. Next, write the correct rule number from the list below in the second blank. Finally, write the possessive form of each noun as singular possessive or as plural possessive.

1. For a singular noun - add (**'s**) Rule 1: girl's	2. For a plural noun that ends in **s** - add (**'**) Rule 2: girls'	3. For a plural noun that does not end in **s** - add (**'s**) Rule 3: women's	
Noun	**S-P**	**Rule**	**Singular Possessive**	**Plural Possessive**
1. tree				
2. candles				
3. dress				
4. postmen				

Chapter 15, Lesson 3, Practice 1: Number 1-9 on a sheet of paper. Write the answers to the questions listed below.

1. What are the three article adjectives?
2. What is an exclamatory sentence?
3. What is a declarative sentence?
4. What is an interrogative sentence?
5. What punctuation mark does a possessive noun always have?
6. What is the abbreviation used for a possessive noun?
7. What is the definition of a pronoun?
8. Name the seven subject pronouns.
9. Name the seven possessive pronouns.

Chapter 15, Lesson 3, Practice 2: First, identify each noun as singular or plural by writing **S** or **P** in the first blank. Next, write the correct rule number from the list below in the second blank. Finally, write the possessive form of each noun as singular possessive or as plural possessive.

1. For a singular noun - add (**'s**) Rule 1: girl's	2. For a plural noun that ends in **s** - add (**'**) Rule 2: girls'	3. For a plural noun that does not end in **s** - add (**'s**) Rule 3: women's	
Noun	**S-P**	**Rule**	**Singular Possessive**	**Plural Possessive**
1. man				
2. nurses				
3. women				
4. shadow				
5. Austin				
6. pillows				

Chapter 16, Lesson 1, Practice 1: First, identify each noun as singular or plural by writing **S** or **P** in the first blank. Next, write the correct rule number from the list below in the second blank. Finally, write the possessive form of each noun as singular possessive or as plural possessive.

1. For a singular noun - add (**'s**)	2. For a plural noun that ends in **s** - add (**'**)	3. For a plural noun that does not end in **s** - add (**'s**)
Rule 1: girl's	Rule 2: girls'	Rule 3: women's

Noun	S-P	Rule	Singular Possessive	Plural Possessive
1. king				
2. olives				
3. Matthew				
4. costume				
5. children				
6. sleeves				

Chapter 16, Lesson 1, Practice 2: Correct the capitalization and punctuation mistakes. Write the rule numbers above the capitalization corrections and below the punctuation corrections. Use Reference 24 for the capitalization rules and Reference 26 for the punctuation rules. The references are located on pages 18 and 19 in your Reference Section.

_____ (capitalization rule numbers)

1. i   have   a   rabbit   named   peter   (Editing Guide: 2 capitals & 1 punctuation)

_____ (punctuation rule numbers)

Chapter 16, Lesson 2, Practice 1: Copy the following words on another sheet of paper. Write the correct contraction beside each word.

Words: he is, who is, there is, we are, were not, did not, let us, I am, she is, they are.

Chapter 16, Lesson 2, Practice 2: Copy the following contractions on another sheet of paper. Write the correct word beside each contraction.

Contractions: isn't, it's, who's, there's, you're, wasn't, don't, can't, doesn't, she's.

Level 2—Shurley English—Homeschool Edition

Chapter 16, Lesson 2, Practice 3: First, identify each noun as singular or plural by writing **S** or **P** in the first blank. Next, write the correct rule number from the list below in the second blank. Finally, write the possessive form of each noun as singular possessive or as plural possessive.

1. For a singular noun - add (**'s**)	2. For a plural noun that ends in **s** - add (**'**)	3. For a plural noun that does not end in **s** - add (**'s**)
Rule 1: girl's	Rule 2: girls'	Rule 3: women's

Noun	S-P	Rule	Singular Possessive	Plural Possessive
1. stems				
2. visitors				
3. wagon				
4. children				
5. waitress				
6. Allen				

Chapter 16, Lesson 3, Practice 1: Copy the following words on another sheet of paper. Write the correct contraction beside each word.

<u>Words</u>: has not, she has, I have, we have, had not, you had, they had, I will, he will, you will, they will, would not, she would, should not.

Chapter 16, Lesson 3, Practice 2: Copy the following contractions on another sheet of paper. Write the correct word beside each contraction.

<u>Contractions</u>: he's, we've, he'd, won't, we'll, you'd, they'd, couldn't, I'll, they'll, hadn't, haven't, hasn't, shouldn't.

Chapter 16, Lesson 3, Practice 3: First, identify each noun as singular or plural by writing **S** or **P** in the first blank. Next, write the correct rule number from the list below in the second blank. Finally, write the possessive form of each noun as singular possessive or as plural possessive.

1. For a singular noun - add (**'s**)	2. For a plural noun that ends in **s** - add (**'**)	3. For a plural noun that does not end in **s** - add (**'s**)
Rule 1: girl's	Rule 2: girls'	Rule 3: women's

Noun	S-P	Rule	Singular Possessive	Plural Possessive
1. zebra				
2. packages				
3. Paul				
4. men				
5. postman				

Chapter 17, Lesson 1, Practice 1: Copy the following words on another sheet of paper. Write the correct contraction beside each word.

Words: let us, was not, there is, you have, has not, should not, they are, you will, I would, will not, have not, did not, I will.

Chapter 17, Lesson 1, Practice 2: Copy the following contractions on another sheet of paper. Write the correct word beside each contraction.

Contractions: it's, I'm, they'll, doesn't, didn't, you're, can't, couldn't, hadn't, who's, he's, we'd, let's, they're, isn't.

Chapter 17, Lesson 2, Practice 1: Copy the following words on another sheet of paper. Write the correct contraction beside each word.

Words: who is, what is, you are, was not, does not, let us, he is, we have, she would, will not, you will, I had, could not.

Chapter 17, Lesson 2, Practice 2: Copy the following contractions on another sheet of paper. Write the correct word beside each contraction.

Contractions: I'm, isn't, it's, aren't, wasn't, don't, can't, he's, haven't, they've, I'll, she'd, shouldn't.

Chapter 17, Lesson 2, Practice 3: Write the correct answer for each sentence.

1. Who is first in line? _____
2. You'll need a jacket. _____
3. He has not worked today. _____
4. You weren't in class today. _____
5. She will visit her aunt. _____
6. I'm taller than Jason is. _____
7. It is raining outside. _____
8. We thought they'd be gone. _____

Chapter 17, Lesson 3, Practice 1: Copy the following words on another sheet of paper. Write the correct contraction beside each word.

Words: he has, who is, there is, we are, were not, did not, let us, she is, you have, had not, he will, we will.

Chapter 17, Lesson 3, Practice 2: Copy the following contractions on another sheet of paper. Write the correct word beside each contraction.

Contractions: isn't, it's, what's, we're, don't, can't, I've, he'd, we'd, I'll, wouldn't, won't, shouldn't.

Level 2—Shurley English—Homeschool Edition

Chapter 17, Lesson 3, Practice 3: Write the correct answer for each sentence.

1. I shouldn't swim alone. _____
2. They are on a ship. _____
3. You have two dollars left. _____
4. What is your name? _____
5. I didn't see you yesterday. _____
6. It is a great party! _____

Chapter 17, Lesson 3, Practice 4: First, identify each noun as singular or plural by writing **S** or **P** in the first blank. Next, write the correct rule number from the list below in the second blank. Finally, write the possessive form of each noun as singular possessive or as plural possessive.

1. For a singular noun - add (**'s**)	2. For a plural noun that ends in **s** - add (**'**)	3. For a plural noun that does not end in **s** - add (**'s**)
Rule 1: girl's	Rule 2: girls'	Rule 3: women's

Noun	S-P	Rule	Singular Possessive	Plural Possessive
1. castle				
2. cashiers				
3. James				
4. men				
5. maps				

Chapter 18, Lesson 1, Practice 1: On notebook paper, make each fragment below into a complete sentence. Underline the parts you add.

1. Add a subject part to this fragment: **rolled down the hill**
2. Add a predicate part to this fragment: **The brilliant scientist**

Chapter 18, Lesson 1, Practice 2: Identify each kind of sentence by writing the abbreviation in the blank. (S, F)

_____ 1. The horses trotted.
_____ 2. Around the corner of the building.
_____ 3. The sweater shrank in the wash.
_____ 4. Mowing my neighbor's yard.
_____ 5. The poster on the wall in my room.

Chapter 18, Lesson 1, Practice 3: Match each subject part with the correct predicate part by writing the correct sentence number in the blank.

	Subject Parts		Predicate Parts
1.	Our pumpkin pie	_____	performed many tricks.
2.	The dry leaves	_____	has five bedrooms.
3.	Our new house	_____	marched in the parade.
4.	The school band	_____	baked in the oven.
5.	The talented magician	_____	fluttered to the ground.

Chapter 18, Lesson 2, Practice 1: Underline the correct homonym in each sentence.

1. We walked (through, threw) the museum.
2. John (knew, new) how to get there.
3. We have one more (weak, week) until vacation.
4. The class had (to, too, two) new students.
5. The king (sent, scent) his jester away.
6. She handed me a (piece, peace) of candy.

Chapter 18, Lesson 2, Practice 2: Copy the following words on another sheet of paper. Write the correct contraction beside each word.

<u>Words:</u> they have, she is, did not, they are, what is, he has, should not, he would, will not, I had, have not, cannot.

Chapter 18, Lesson 2, Practice 3: On notebook paper, make each fragment below into a complete sentence. Underline the parts you add.

1. Add a subject part to this fragment: **turned into a beast**
2. Add a predicate part to this fragment: **The crowd of people**

Chapter 18, Lesson 2, Practice 4: Identify each kind of sentence by writing the abbreviation in the blank. (S, F)

_____ 1. The tulips bloomed.
_____ 2. The cool water rushed through the creek bed.
_____ 3. The voice on the radio.
_____ 4. The workers moved the heavy boxes.
_____ 5. Through the winter storm.

Level 2—Shurley English—Homeschool Edition

Chapter 18, Lesson 2, Practice 5: Match each subject part with the correct predicate part by writing the correct sentence number in the blank.

	Subject Parts		**Predicate Parts**
1.	Mom's beautiful painting	_____	drank the milk.
2.	The little kitten	_____	were empty.
3.	The gentle nurse	_____	took pictures at the wedding.
4.	Both cardboard boxes	_____	hangs on the wall.
5.	The photographer	_____	took my temperature.

Chapter 18, Lesson 3, Practice 1: On notebook paper, make each fragment below into a complete sentence. Underline the parts you add.

1. Add a subject part to this fragment: **worked in the garden**
2. Add a predicate part to this fragment: **The silver coin**

Chapter 18, Lesson 3, Practice 2: Identify each kind of sentence by writing the abbreviation in the blank. (S, F)

_____ 1. By the new grocery store.
_____ 2. Waiting patiently in the den.
_____ 3. The ice melted in my glass.
_____ 4. Ran around in circles.
_____ 5. The tree swayed in the wind.

Chapter 18, Lesson 3, Practice 3: Match each subject part with the correct predicate part by writing the correct sentence number in the blank.

	Subject Parts		**Predicate Parts**
1.	The old chair	_____	chewed on bamboo.
2.	My throat	_____	collapsed under me.
3.	The postman	_____	stamped the packages.
4.	The dance rehearsal	_____	feels sore.
5.	The panda	_____	lasted for hours.

Chapter 18, Lesson 3, Practice 4: Copy the following contractions on another sheet of paper. Write the correct word beside each contraction.

<u>**Contractions:**</u> hasn't, you've, he'd, won't, we'll, she'd, couldn't, it's, aren't, weren't, let's, wasn't.

Chapter 19, Lesson 1, Practice 1: On notebook paper, make each fragment below into a complete sentence. Underline the parts you add.

1. Add a subject part to this fragment: **waded into the ocean**
2. Add a predicate part to this fragment: **The gold medal**

Chapter 19, Lesson 1, Practice 2: Identify each kind of sentence by writing the abbreviation in the blank. (S, F)

_____ 1. Near the edge of the water.

_____ 2. We played violins in the orchestra.

_____ 3. A bag of chocolate candy.

_____ 4. Fell down the stairs.

_____ 5. The tiger jumped through the burning hoop.

Chapter 19, Lesson 1, Practice 3: Match each subject part with the correct predicate part by writing the correct sentence number in the blank.

Subject Parts	Predicate Parts
1. The onions	_____ fits well.
2. The gray rat	_____ melted in my lap.
3. Several dark clouds	_____ nibbled on a piece of cheese.
4. My new suit	_____ made my eyes burn.
5. The ice cream sundae	_____ covered the sky.

Chapter 19, Lesson 1, Practice 4: Copy the following words on another sheet of paper. Write the correct contraction beside each word.

Words: did not, we are, who is, I am, she had, you will, we would, they have, she has, let us, cannot, it is.

Chapter 19, Lesson 2, Practice 1: On notebook paper, make each fragment below into a complete sentence. Underline the parts you add.

1. Add a subject part to this fragment: **painted a picture**
2. Add a predicate part to this fragment: **The colorful rainbow**

Chapter 19, Lesson 2, Practice 2: Identify each kind of sentence by writing the abbreviation in the blank. (S, F)

_____ 1. The children built a snowman.
_____ 2. Joey and Matt hiked up the trail.
_____ 3. Delivered the papers daily.
_____ 4. The thick mane on the lion's head.
_____ 5. Our yard was filled with yellow dandelions.

Chapter 19, Lesson 2, Practice 3: Match each subject part with the correct predicate part by writing the correct sentence number in the blank.

Subject Parts	**Predicate Parts**
1. The little girl's blue dress	_____ shattered into pieces.
2. My dresser mirror	_____ had ruffles.
3. The boy's shoelaces	_____ served hamburgers for lunch.
4. Our school cafeteria	_____ had long horns.
5. John's goat	_____ were tied in knots.

Chapter 19, Lesson 2, Practice 4: For each sentence, do these four things: (1) Write the subject. (2) Write **S** if the subject is singular or **P** if the subject is plural. (3) Write the rule number. (4) Underline the correct verb in the sentence.

Rule 1: A singular subject must use a singular verb form that ends in **s**: _is, was, has, does,_ or verbs ending with **es**.
Rule 2: A plural subject, a compound subject, or the subject **YOU** must use a plural verb form that has **no s** ending: _are, were, do, have,_ or verbs without **s** or **es** endings. (A plural verb form is also called the _plain form._)

Subject	**S or P**	**Rule**	
			1. The green lizard (chase, chases) the grasshopper.
			2. A crab (pinch, pinches) my toe.
			3. The girls (wear, wears) ribbons in their hair.
			4. The ship (sail, sails) across the ocean.
			5. Robin and Lisa (shiver, shivers) in the cold.
			6. You (tie, ties) your shoes.

Chapter 19, Lesson 3, Practice 1: Use the following guidelines to make each noun possessive. First, identify each noun as singular or plural by writing **S** or **P** in the first blank. Next, write the correct rule number from the list below in the second blank. Finally, write the possessive form of each noun as singular possessive or as plural possessive.

1. For a singular noun - add ('s)	2. For a plural noun that ends in *s* - add (')	3. For a plural noun that does not end in *s* - add ('s)
Rule 1: girl's	Rule 2: girls'	Rule 3: women's

Noun	S-P	Rule	Singular Possessive	Plural Possessive
1. towers				
2. worm				
3. children				
4. melons				
5. Kelly				

Chapter 19, Lesson 3, Practice 2: Match each subject part with the correct predicate part by writing the correct sentence number in the blank.

Subject Parts

1. My wrinkled shirt
2. Two lifeguards
3. A handsome prince
4. The jelly jar
5. A wasp

Predicate Parts

_____ was made of glass.
_____ watched the children swim.
_____ stung my arm.
_____ rescued the princess.
_____ needs to be ironed.

Chapter 19, Lesson 3, Practice 3: Identify each kind of sentence by writing the abbreviation in the blank. (S, F)

_____ 1. Through the hole in the door.
_____ 2. I made a strawberry milkshake.
_____ 3. Ticking loudly on the wall.
_____ 4. The stranger asked for a dollar.
_____ 5. Up the rocky hill.

Chapter 19, Lesson 3, Practice 4: On notebook paper, make each fragment below into a complete sentence. Underline the parts you add.

1. Add a subject part to this fragment: **skated across the pond**
2. Add a predicate part to this fragment: **The shaggy dog**

Chapter 19, Lesson 3, Practice 5: Correct the capitalization and punctuation mistakes. Write the rule numbers above the capitalization corrections and below the punctuation corrections. Use Reference 24 for the capitalization rules and Reference 26 for the punctuation rules. The references are located on pages 18 and 19 in your Reference Section.

_____ (Capitalization Rule numbers)

1. i went to a conference in ft collins colorado (Editing Guide: 4 capitals & 3 punctuation)

_____ (Punctuation Rule numbers)

Chapter 20, Lesson 1, Practice: Identify the tense of each underlined verb by writing a number **1** for present tense, a number **2** for past tense, and a number **3** for future tense.

Verb Tense	Verbs	Verb Tense	Verbs
	1. He played the trombone.		4. The teams rest after the long game.
	2. He plays the trombone.		5. The teams will rest after the long game.
	3. He will play the trombone.		6. The teams rested after the long game.

Chapter 20, Lesson 3, Practice: Identify the tense of each underlined verb by writing a number **1** for present tense, a number **2** for past tense, and a number **3** for future tense. Use the verb chart for the irregular verbs.

Verb Tense	Regular Verbs	Verb Tense	Irregular Verbs
	1. The crowd will bow to the king.		9. Steven drove a truck.
	2. The crowd bowed to the king.		10. Steven drives a truck.
	3. The crowd bows to the king.		11. Steven will drive a truck.
	4. The ice melts in her glass.		12. I ate a piece of her cake.
	5. The ice will melt in her glass.		13. I will eat a piece of her cake.
	6. I lock the bolt on the door.		14. The dog digs a hole to hide his bone.
	7. I will lock the bolt on the door.		15. The dog will dig a hole to hide his bone.
	8. I locked the bolt on the door.		16. The dog dug a hole to hide his bone.

Chapter 21, Lesson 1, Practice 1: Identify the tense of each underlined verb by writing a number **1** for present tense, a number **2** for past tense, and a number **3** for future tense. Use the verb chart for the irregular verbs.

Verb Tense	Regular Verbs	Verb Tense	Irregular Verbs
	1. The dogs chased the rabbits.		9. Jacob shakes his wrapped present.
	2. The dogs chase the rabbits.		10. Jacob will shake his wrapped present.
	3. The dogs will chase the rabbits.		11. Jacob shook his wrapped present.
	4. My dad shaved his beard.		12. The bell will ring at the end of class.
	5. My dad will shave his beard.		13. The bell rang at the end of class.
	6. My dad shaves his beard.		14. The bell rings at the end of class.
	7. Jim showed me his new bike.		15. Marshall will come to the party.
	8. Jim will show me his new bike.		16. Marshall came to the party.

Level 2—Shurley English—Homeschool Edition

Chapter 21, Lesson 1, Practice 2: Copy the following words on notebook paper. Write the correct contraction beside each word.

Words: is not, it is, that is, there is, you are, they are, do not, did not, let us, I have.

Chapter 21, Lesson 1, Practice 3: Copy the following contractions on notebook paper. Write the correct word beside each contraction.

Contractions: couldn't, they'd, we'll, you'd, I've, she's, can't, doesn't, he's, I'm.

Chapter 21, Lesson 2, Practice: Identify the tense of each underlined verb by writing a number **1** for present tense, a number **2** for past tense, and a number **3** for future tense. Use the verb chart for the irregular verbs.

Verb Tense	Regular Verbs	Verb Tense	Irregular Verbs
	1. We <u>skated</u> down the hill.		9. The class <u>will take</u> the exam.
	2. We <u>skate</u> down the hill.		10. The class <u>takes</u> the exam.
	3. We <u>will skate</u> down the hill.		11. The class <u>took</u> the exam.
	4. I <u>stepped</u> over the mud puddle.		12. The sun <u>rises</u> in the east.
	5. I <u>will step</u> over the mud puddle.		13. The sun <u>rose</u> in the east.
	6. I <u>step</u> over the mud puddle.		14. The sun <u>will rise</u> in the east.
	7. The zookeeper <u>will touch</u> the snake.		15. The Smiths <u>sold</u> their house.
	8. The zookeeper <u>touches</u> the snake.		16. The Smiths <u>will sell</u> their house.

Chapter 21, Lesson 3, Practice: Identify the tense of each underlined verb by writing a number **1** for present tense, a number **2** for past tense, and a number **3** for future tense. Use the verb chart for the irregular verbs.

Verb Tense	Regular Verbs	Verb Tense	Irregular Verbs
	1. The actors <u>danced</u> across the stage.		6. We <u>will swim</u> in the hotel's pool.
	2. The actors <u>dance</u> across the stage.		7. We <u>swam</u> in the hotel's pool.
	3. The actors <u>will dance</u> across the stage.		8. We <u>swim</u> in the hotel's pool.
	4. My costume <u>scared</u> Rita.		9. Angela <u>made</u> a quilt.
	5. My costume <u>will scare</u> Rita.		10. Angela <u>makes</u> a quilt.

Chapter 22, Lesson 2, Practice 1: Write the parts of a friendly letter in the correct places in the friendly letter below.

1. **Heading** 2. **Greeting** 3. **Closing** 4. **Signature**

23 Diamond Drive   Dear Teresa,   Your friend,   Emily
Somerset, KY 26400
July 9, 20___

5. **Body**

My dog had five puppies today. Two of them have spots. They are all so cute!

Friendly Letter

Chapter 22, Lesson 2, Practice 2: Use the information in Chapter 22, Lesson 2, Practice 1 to match the definitions. Write the correct letter of the word beside each definition.

_____	1. person who wrote the letter	A.	Your friend,
_____	2. person who will receive the letter	B.	Emily's new puppies
_____	3. when the letter was written	C.	Teresa
_____	4. where the writer lives	D.	July 9, 20___
_____	5. the closing	E.	Dear Teresa,
_____	6. the greeting	F.	Emily
_____	7. what this letter is about	G.	23 Diamond Drive, Somerset, KY 26400

Chapter 22, Lesson 2, Practice 3

Write a friendly letter to a neighbor, nursing home resident, or relative. Before you start, review the references and tips for writing friendly letters. After your letter has been checked for mistakes, fold the letter and put it in an envelope.

Chapter 22, Lesson 3, Practice 1: Write the parts of a friendly letter in the correct places in the friendly letter below.

1. **Heading**
   13 West Plains Drive
   Casper, WY 56400
   May 22, 20____

2. **Greeting**
   Dear Aunt Kathy,

3. **Closing**
   Your niece,

4. **Signature**
   Gloria

5. **Body**
   Mom's birthday is next month, and I am having trouble finding the perfect gift. Do you have any ideas?

Friendly Letter

Chapter 22, Lesson 3, Practice 2

Write a friendly letter to a special friend or relative. Before you start, review the references and tips for writing friendly letters. After your letter has been edited, fold the letter and put it in an envelope.

Chapter 23, Lesson 2, Practice 1: Fill in the blanks on the envelope with the sample parts below. Draw a stamp in the proper place on the envelope.

Sample Parts of an Envelope:

1. Emily Thompson (writer)
   23 Diamond Drive
   Somerset, KY 26400

2. Teresa Lewis (receiver)
   160 Lemon Street
   Macon, GA 53100

Envelope

Chapter 23, Lesson 2, Practice 2: Use the information in Chapter 23, Lesson 2, Practice 1 to match the definitions. Write the correct letter of the word beside each definition.

_____ 1. person who wrote the letter   A. 160 Lemon Street, Macon, GA 53100

_____ 2. person who will receive the letter   B. Teresa Lewis

_____ 3. where the writer lives   C. Emily Thompson

_____ 4. where the person receiving the letter lives   D. 23 Diamond Drive,
                                                           Somerset, KY 26400

Chapter 23, Lesson 3, Practice 1: Fill in the blanks on the envelope with the sample parts below. Draw a stamp in the proper place on the envelope.

Sample Parts of an Envelope:

1. Gloria Peterson (writer)
   13 West Plains Drive
   Casper, WY 56400

2. Kathy Peterson (receiver)
   244 Georgia Street
   Fresno, CA 67800

Envelope

Chapter 23, Lesson 3, Practice 2: Use the information in Chapter 23, Lesson 3, Practice 1 to match the definitions. Write the correct letter of the word beside each definition.

____ 1. person who wrote the letter   A. Kathy Peterson

____ 2. person who will receive the letter   B. Gloria Peterson

____ 3. where the writer lives   C. 244 Georgia Street, Fresno, CA 67800

____ 4. where the person receiving the letter lives   D. 13 West Plains Drive,
                                                          Casper, WY 56400

Chapter 23, Lesson 3, Practice 3

Write a friendly letter to a special friend or relative. Before you start, review the references and tips for writing friendly letters. After your letter has been edited, fold the letter and put it in an envelope. Address the envelope properly and mail it. Don't forget the stamp.

Chapter 24, Lesson 1, Practice

Write your own thank-you note. First, think of a person who has done something nice for you or has given you a gift (even the gift of time). Next, write that person a thank-you note, using the information in the Reference Section as a guide.

Chapter 24, Lesson 2, Practice

Write another thank-you note. First, think of a person who has done something nice for you or has given you a gift (even the gift of time). Next, write that person a thank-you note, using the information in the Reference Section as a guide.

Chapter 25, Lesson 3, Practice: Underline the correct answer in each sentence.

1. Nonfiction books contain information and stories that are (true, not true).

2. Fiction books contain information and stories that are (true, not true).

3. The most common reference books are the dictionary and the encyclopedia. (true, not true)

Chapter 26, Lesson 1, Practice: Underline the correct homonym in each sentence.

1. The package was (sent, scent) yesterday.
2. It is (to, too, two) cold outside.
3. I (new, knew) that I was wrong.
4. (Right, Write) your birthday on my calendar.
5. Mark (through, threw) his jacket on the couch.
6. The drivers quickly finished the (course, coarse).

Chapter 26, Lesson 2, Practice 1: Match each part of a book listed below with the type of information it may give you. Write the appropriate letter in the blank. You may use each letter only once.

A. Index   B. Appendix   C. Bibliography   D. Preface   E. Body   F. Copyright page

1. ____ Reason the book was written

2. ____ Text of the book

3. ____ ISBN number

4. ____ Exact page numbers for a particular topic and used to locate topics quickly

5. ____ Extra maps in a book

6. ____ Books listed for finding more information

Chapter 26, Lesson 2, Practice 2

On notebook paper, write the five parts found at the front of a book.

Chapter 26, Lesson 2, Practice 3

On notebook paper, write the four parts found at the back of a book.

Chapter 26, Lesson 3, Practice

Write the nine parts of a book on a poster and write a description beside each part. Illustrate and color the nine parts.

TEST

SECTION

Level 2—Shurley English—Homeschool Edition

Chapter 1 Test

Exercise 1: Write the letters in each group below in alphabetical order.

1. n z f c _____

2. p d v h _____

3. c x k o u r _____

4. w g l t e z b m _____

Exercise 2: Put each group of words in alphabetical order. Use numbers to show the order in each column.

Space Words	Color Words	"G" Words
_____ 1. astronaut	_____ 3. black	_____ 5. grape
_____ 2. moon	_____ 4. brown	_____ 6. glaze

Exercise 3: Put each group of words in alphabetical order. Use numbers to show the order in each column.

Hospital Words	"O" Words	Fruit Words
_____ 1. patient	_____ 4. ostrich	_____ 7. mango
_____ 2. doctor	_____ 5. omelet	_____ 8. peach
_____ 3. nurse	_____ 6. olive	_____ 9. pear

Exercise 4: Put each group of words in alphabetical order. Use numbers to show the order in each column.

Movie Words	"L" Words	"V" Words
_____ 1. popcorn	_____ 5. laugh	_____ 9. velvet
_____ 2. previews	_____ 6. light	_____ 10. value
_____ 3. candy	_____ 7. leopard	_____ 11. view
_____ 4. soda	_____ 8. language	_____ 12. vanish

Exercise 5: In your journal, write a paragraph summarizing what you have learned this week.

Chapter 2 Test

Exercise 1: Classify each sentence.

1.   Carpenters   worked.

2.   Horse   trotted.

Exercise 2: Put the letters below in alphabetical order.

1. t d n o z a w p _____

Exercise 3: Put each group of words in alphabetical order. Use numbers 1-4 in the blanks to show the order in each column.

Winter Words	Plant Words	"R" Words
_____ 1. coat	_____ 5. leaf	_____ 9. rabbit
_____ 2. snow	_____ 6. stem	_____ 10. roll
_____ 3. mittens	_____ 7. flower	_____ 11. right
_____ 4. ice	_____ 8. root	_____ 12. ready

Exercise 4: Identify each pair of words as synonyms or antonyms by putting parentheses ( ) around **syn** or **ant**.

1. eager, enthusiastic	syn ant	3. impolite, respectful	syn ant
2. crawl, gallop	syn ant	4. tribute, salute	syn ant

Exercise 5: Match the definitions. Write the correct letter beside each numbered concept.

_____ 1. verb question   A. person, place, or thing

_____ 2. subject-noun question (thing)   B. who

_____ 3. parts of a complete sentence   C. a capital letter

_____ 4. noun   D. subject, verb, complete sense

_____ 5. subject-noun question (person)   E. what

_____ 6. sentences should begin with   F. sentence

_____ 7. tells what the subject does   G. what is being said about

_____ 8. ends with an end mark   H. verb

Exercise 6: In your journal, write a paragraph summarizing what you have learned this week.

Level 2—Shurley English—Homeschool Edition

Chapter 3 Test

Exercise 1: Classify each sentence.

1. Four   brown   squirrels   looked   cautiously   around.

2. Six   firemen   worked   carefully.

Exercise 2: Name the four parts of speech that you have studied. (*You may use abbreviations.*)

1. _____   2. _____   3. _____   4. _____

Exercise 3: Identify each pair of words as synonyms or antonyms by putting parentheses ( ) around **syn** or **ant**.					
1. splendid, magnificent	syn ant	3. brisk, sluggish	syn ant	5. enthusiastic, eager	syn ant
2. impolite, respectful	syn ant	4. soar, fly	syn ant	6. hasty, cautious	syn ant

Exercise 4: Write *a* or *an* in the blanks.
1. Molly saw _____ squirrel today.
2. He was _____ astronaut.
3. They own _____ ostrich.
4. She is _____ nurse.
5. We have _____ easy job.
6. He wants _____ trumpet.
7. ___ organ
8. ___ sack
9. ___ item
10. ___ rabbit
11. ___ outlet
12. ___ bath

Exercise 5: Match the definitions. Write the correct letter beside each numbered concept.

_____ 1. sentences should begin with   A. subject, verb, complete sense
_____ 2. adjective modifies   B. verb, adjective, or adverb
_____ 3. verb question   C. noun or pronoun
_____ 4. tells what the subject does   D. verb
_____ 5. subject-noun question (thing)   E. who
_____ 6. parts of a complete sentence   F. what is being said about
_____ 7. noun   G. person, place, or thing
_____ 8. subject-noun question (person)   H. what
_____ 9. adverb modifies   I. capital letter

Exercise 6: In your journal, write a paragraph summarizing what you have learned this week.

Chapter 4 Test

Exercise 1: Classify each sentence.

1. The huge military plane flew low today.

2. The crisp morning air blew gently.

Exercise 2: Identify each pair of words as synonyms or antonyms by putting parentheses ( ) around **syn** or **ant**.

1. clumsy, graceful	syn ant	4. cautious, hasty	syn ant	7. often, frequent	syn ant
2. suspend, dangle	syn ant	5. antique, modern	syn ant	8. enthusiastic, eager	syn ant
3. salute, tribute	syn ant	6. gallop, crawl	syn ant	9. soar, fly	syn ant

Exercise 3: Put the end mark and the abbreviation for each kind of sentence in the blanks below.

1. Mom's favorite vase tumbled off the top shelf _____

2. What was the answer to her question _____

3. Will you wash the dishes _____

4. My new shoes are brown _____

Exercise 4: Match the definitions. Write the correct letter beside each numbered concept.

_____ 1. subject-noun question (person)	A. a, an, the
_____ 2. verb question	B. verb
_____ 3. article adjectives	C. noun marker
_____ 4. sentences should begin with	D. what
_____ 5. adverb modifies	E. verb, adjective, or adverb
_____ 6. noun	F. subject, verb, complete sense
_____ 7. article adjective can be called	G. person, place, or thing
_____ 8. subject-noun question (thing)	H. who
_____ 9. adjective modifies	I. noun or pronoun
_____ 10. tells what the subject does	J. what is being said about
_____ 11. parts of a complete sentence	K. a capital letter

Exercise 5: Write *a* or *an* in the blanks.

1. Jim went to ____ auction.   3. He flew ____ airplane.   5. ____ battery   7. ____ spoon

2. Peter baked ____ pizza.   4. The queen wore ____ crown.   6. ____ star   8. ____ orchid

Exercise 6: Name the four parts of speech that you have studied. (*You may use abbreviations.*)

1. _____   2. _____   3. _____   4. _____

Exercise 7: In your journal, write a paragraph summarizing what you have learned this week.

Chapter 5 Test

Exercise 1: Classify each sentence.

1. Wild ducks descend gracefully.

2. The thick, annoying smoke drifted upward.

Exercise 2: Identify each pair of words as synonyms or antonyms by putting parentheses ( ) around **syn** or **ant**.

1. often, frequent	syn ant	4. annoy, irritate	syn ant	7. disappear, vanish	syn ant
2. excited, calm	syn ant	5. antique, modern	syn ant	8. dangle, suspend	syn ant
3. soar, fly	syn ant	6. mournful, delightful	syn ant	9. graceful, clumsy	syn ant

Exercise 3: Put the end mark and the abbreviation for each kind of sentence in the blanks below.

1. James tripped over the water hose _____

2. The waiter poured the coffee _____

3. Do you have a pet rabbit _____

Exercise 4: For each noun listed below, write **C** for common or **P** for proper.

Noun	C or P	Noun	C or P	Noun	C or P
1. Walter		4. city		7. yellow	
2. St. Peter		5. tuna		8. poster	
3. painting		6. Texas		9. Paula	

Exercise 5: For each noun listed below, write **S** for singular or **P** for plural.

Noun	S or P	Noun	S or P	Noun	S or P
1. board		4. stores		7. matches	
2. dress		5. birds		8. nails	
3. planets		6. brother		9. spider	

Exercise 6: Write *a* or *an* in the blanks.

1. That is ____ adorable puppy.   3. She made ____ mistake.   5. ____ point   7. ____ ounce

2. Chad listened for ____ echo.   4. Sewing is ____ hobby.   6. ____ approval   8. ____ gym

Exercise 7: Name the four parts of speech that you have studied. (*You may use abbreviations.*)

1. _____   2. _____   3. _____   4. _____

Exercise 8: In your journal, write a paragraph summarizing what you have learned this week.

Level 2—Shurley English—Homeschool Edition

Chapter 6 Test

Exercise 1: Classify each sentence.

1. The thick fog disappeared rapidly today.

2. The fresh hot pizza arrived unexpectedly.

Exercise 2: Use Sentence 2 to underline the complete subject once and the complete predicate twice and to complete the table below.					
List the Noun Used	List the Noun Job	Singular or Plural	Common or Proper	Simple Subject	Simple Predicate
1.	2.	3.	4.	5.	6.

Exercise 3: Identify each pair of words as synonyms or antonyms by putting parentheses ( ) around *syn* or *ant*.					
1. irritate, annoy	syn ant	4. disappear, vanish	syn ant	7. scamper, scurry	syn ant
2. brilliant, dull	syn ant	5. simple, complex	syn ant	8. frequent, often	syn ant
3. anger, rage	syn ant	6. mournful, delightful	syn ant	9. excited, calm	syn ant

Exercise 4: Put the end mark and the abbreviation for each kind of sentence in the blanks below.

1. My new shoes are covered in mud _____

2. The bread is on the cabinet _____

3. May I help you _____

Exercise 5: Write **S** for singular or **P** for plural.	
Noun	**S or P**
1. paper	
2. voices	
3. swing	

Exercise 6: Write **C** for Common or **P** for proper.	
Noun	**C or P**
1. Mississippi	
2. George	
3. patio	

Exercise 7: Write *a* or *an* in the blanks.

1. Uncle Joe owns ____ motel.   3. The priest said ____ prayer.   5. ____ wolf   7. ____ hunter

2. We did ____ activity.   4. The ship dropped ____ anchor.   6. ____ axe   8. ____ ostrich

Exercise 8: Name the four parts of speech that you have studied. (*You may use abbreviations.*)

1. _____   2. _____   3. _____   4. _____

Exercise 9: In your journal, write a paragraph summarizing what you have learned this week.

Chapter 7 Test

Exercise 1: Classify each sentence.

1. _____ The antique copper teakettle whistled loudly.

2. _____ A little brown snail crawled slowly away.

Exercise 2: Use Sentence 1 to underline the complete subject once and the complete predicate twice and to complete the table below.					
List the Noun Used	List the Noun Job	Singular or Plural	Common or Proper	Simple Subject	Simple Predicate
1.	2.	3.	4.	5.	6.

Exercise 3: Identify each pair of words as synonyms or antonyms by putting parentheses ( ) around **syn** or **ant**.					
1. annoy, irritate	syn ant	4. above, overhead	syn ant	7. disappear, vanish	syn ant
2. depart, arrive	syn ant	5. complex, simple	syn ant	8. freight, cargo	syn ant
3. graceful, clumsy	syn ant	6. collapse, build	syn ant	9. brilliant, dull	syn ant

Exercise 4: Write **S** for singular or **P** for plural.	
Noun	S or P
1. mice	
2. windows	
3. caterpillar	

Exercise 5: Write **C** for Common or **P** for proper.	
Noun	C or P
1. Sandy	
2. pepper	
3. December	

Exercise 6: Write *a* or *an* in the blanks.

1. We heard ___ strange voice.   3. This is ___ bitter apple.   5. ___ glass   7. ___ arm

2. Three is ___ odd number.   4. Kelly is ___ only child.   6. ___ watch   8. ___ octopus

Exercise 7: Name the four parts of speech that you have studied. (*You may use abbreviations.*)

1. _____   2. _____   3. _____   4. _____

Exercise 8: In your journal, write a paragraph summarizing what you have learned this week.

Chapter 8 Test

Exercise 1: Classify each sentence.

1. _____ The swim team competed in the finals.

2. _____ The candles flickered softly in the dark.

Exercise 2: Use Sentence 1 to underline the complete subject once and the complete predicate twice and to complete the table below.

List the Noun Used	List the Noun Job	Singular or Plural	Common or Proper	Simple Subject	Simple Predicate
1.	2.	3.	4.	5.	6.
7.	8.	9.	10.		

Exercise 3: Name the five parts of speech that you have studied. (*You may use abbreviations.*)

1. _____ 2. _____ 3. _____ 4. _____ 5. _____

Exercise 4: Identify each pair of words as synonyms or antonyms by putting parentheses ( ) around **syn** or **ant**.

1. flicker, flash	syn ant	4. nibble, munch	syn ant	7. energetic, weary	syn ant
2. depart, arrive	syn ant	5. brilliant, dull	syn ant	8. anger, rage	syn ant
3. scamper, scurry	syn ant	6. build, collapse	syn ant	9. gush, trickle	syn ant

Exercise 5: Write **S** for singular or **P** for plural.

Noun	S or P
1. toads	
2. women	
3. coffee	

Exercise 6: Write **C** for Common or **P** for proper.

Noun	C or P
1. juice	
2. store	
3. Mexico	

Exercise 7: Write *a* or *an* in the blanks.

1. The chef cut ____ onion.   3. Terry lives by ____ swamp.   5. ____ tulip   7. ____ radish

2. We went on ____ walk.   4. Frank planted ____ oak tree.   6. ____ apology   8. ____ castle

Exercise 8: In your journal, write a paragraph summarizing what you have learned this week.

Chapter 9 Test

Exercise 1: Classify each sentence.

1. _____ The frightened student pilot landed carefully on the runway before sundown.

2. _____ The stunt driver plunged fearlessly down the steep hill!

Exercise 2: Use Sentence 1 to underline the complete subject once and the complete predicate twice and to complete the table below.

List the Noun Used	List the Noun Job	Singular or Plural	Common or Proper	Simple Subject	Simple Predicate
1.	2.	3.	4.	5.	6.
7.	8.	9.	10.		
11.	12.	13.	14.		

Exercise 3: Name the five parts of speech that you have studied. (*You may use abbreviations.*)

1. _____ 2. _____ 3. _____ 4. _____ 5. _____

Exercise 4: Identify each pair of words as synonyms or antonyms by putting parentheses ( ) around **syn** or **ant**.

1. plunge, immerse	syn ant	4. collapse, build	syn ant	7. weary, energetic	syn ant
2. gush, trickle	syn ant	5. abandon, keep	syn ant	8. constant, unchanging	syn ant
3. overhead, above	syn ant	6. rage, anger	syn ant	9. expert, beginner	syn ant

Exercise 5: Underline the correct homonym in each sentence.

1. My cold made me feel (weak, week).
2. We placed our jackets over (there, their).
3. I want to (hear, here) the choir sing.
4. He (led, lead) the troops into battle.
5. Mr. Paul (sent, scent) me a birthday card.
6. Christmas is only a (weak, week) away.
7. The state (counsel, council) met yesterday.
8. We lost one (piece, peace) of our puzzle.

Exercise 6: In your journal, write a paragraph summarizing what you have learned this week.

Level 2—Shurley English—Homeschool Edition

Chapter 10 Test

Exercise 1: Classify each sentence.

1. _____ An ugly crocodile lies harmlessly on the bank of the river.

2. _____ Ann rode to school in the yellow bus today.

Exercise 2: Use Sentence 2 to underline the complete subject once and the complete predicate twice and to complete the table below.

List the Noun Used	List the Noun Job	Singular or Plural	Common or Proper	Simple Subject	Simple Predicate
1.	2.	3.	4.	5.	6.
7.	8.	9.	10.		
11.	12.	13.	14.		

Exercise 3: Name the five parts of speech that you have studied. (*You may use abbreviations.*)

1. _____ 2. _____ 3. _____ 4. _____ 5. _____

Exercise 4: Identify each pair of words as synonyms or antonyms by putting parentheses ( ) around **syn** or **ant**.

1. canyon, gorge	syn ant	4. expert, beginner	syn ant	7. nibble, munch	syn ant
2. abandon, keep	syn ant	5. weary, energetic	syn ant	8. bewilder, confuse	syn ant
3. flicker, flash	syn ant	6. youthful, old	syn ant	9. harmless, dangerous	syn ant

Exercise 5: Underline the correct homonym in each sentence.

1. That light is (to, too, two) bright.
2. The quarterback (threw, through) the ball.
3. The perfume had a marvelous (sent, scent).
4. Robert felt (week, weak) after the marathon.

Exercise 6: For each sentence, do these four things: (1) Write the subject. (2) Write **S** if the subject is singular or **P** if the subject is plural. (3) Write the rule number. (4) Underline the correct verb in the sentence.

Rule 1 and Rule 2 are located in Reference 21 on page 17 in your student book.

Subject	S or P	Rule

1. The shelter (provide, provides) dinners for the homeless.
2. The campers (casts, cast) their tent near the fire.
3. The beam (supports, support) the building.
4. The snow (cover, covers) the ground.
5. You (cleans, clean) your room.

Exercise 7: In your journal, write a paragraph summarizing what you have learned this week.

Chapter 11 Test

Exercise 1: Classify each sentence.

1. _____ The young students screamed with delight at the splendid costumes for the parade!

2. _____ The hillside of mixed flowers exploded with brilliant colors.

Exercise 2: Use Sentence 1 to underline the complete subject once and the complete predicate twice and to complete the table below.

List the Noun Used	List the Noun Job	Singular or Plural	Common or Proper	Simple Subject	Simple Predicate
1.	2.	3.	4.	5.	6.
7.	8.	9.	10.		
11.	12.	13.	14.		
15.	16.	17.	18.		

Exercise 3: Name the five parts of speech that you have studied. (*You may use abbreviations.*)

1. _____ 2. _____ 3. _____ 4. _____ 5. _____

Exercise 4: Identify each pair of words as synonyms or antonyms by putting parentheses ( ) around **syn** or **ant**.

1. clog, block	syn ant	4. exhausted, refreshed	syn ant	7. constant, unchanging	syn ant
2. youthful, old	syn ant	5. tardy, punctual	syn ant	8. bewilder, confuse	syn ant
3. alert, aware	syn ant	6. plunge, immerse	syn ant	9. harmless, dangerous	syn ant

Exercise 5: For each sentence, do these four things: (1) Write the subject. (2) Write **S** if the subject is singular or **P** if the subject is plural. (3) Write the rule number. (4) Underline the correct verb in the sentence.

Rule 1 and Rule 2 are located in Reference 21 on page 17 in your student book.

Subject	S or P	Rule	
			1. You (sings, sing) very well.
			2. Bill and Linda (helps, help) their new neighbors.
			3. The clock (chimes, chime) every hour.
			4. The clothes (wrinkles, wrinkle) in the dryer.
			5. The scientist (discovers, discover) a new cure.

Exercise 6: Underline the correct homonym in each sentence.

1. Mallory is my (new, knew) friend.
2. He ran (to, too, two) the finish line.
3. We live by a golf (coarse, course).
4. She (sent, scent) the letter via airmail.

Exercise 7: In your journal, write a paragraph summarizing what you have learned this week.

Chapter 12 Test

Exercise 1: Classify each sentence.

1. _____ The tall, slim elderly man came to the office for an interview.

2. _____ We ran for cover during the storm.

Exercise 2: Use Sentence 2 to underline the complete subject once and the complete predicate twice and to complete the table below.

List the Noun Used	List the Noun Job	Singular or Plural	Common or Proper	Simple Subject	Simple Predicate
1.	2.	3.	4.	5.	6.
7.	8.	9.	10.		

Exercise 3: Name the six parts of speech that you have studied. (*You may use abbreviations.*)

1. _____ 2. _____ 3. _____ 4. _____ 5. _____ 6. _____

Exercise 4: Identify each pair of words as synonyms or antonyms by putting parentheses ( ) around **syn** or **ant**.

1. beneath, below	syn ant	4. tardy, punctual	syn ant	7. canyon, gorge	syn ant
2. waddle, stride	syn ant	5. clog, block	syn ant	8. cranky, grouchy	syn ant
3. aware, alert	syn ant	6. slow, nimble	syn ant	9. exhausted, refreshed	syn ant

Exercise 5: Correct the capitalization mistakes and put the rule number above each correction. Use the rule numbers in Reference 24 on page 18 in the Reference Section of your book.

_____ (capitalization rule numbers)

1. katie and susan live on maple street.   (Editing Guide: 4 capitalization mistakes)

_____ (capitalization rule numbers)

2. miss taylor works in portland, oregon.   (Editing Guide: 4 capitalization mistakes)

Exercise 6: Underline the correct homonym in each sentence.

1. Telling the truth is the (right, write) thing to do.
2. September has thirty (daze, days).
3. The dog chased (its, it's) tail.
4. Sara (new, knew) all fifty states.

Exercise 7: In your journal, write a paragraph summarizing what you have learned this week.

Level 2—Shurley English—Homeschool Edition

Chapter 13 Test

Exercise 1: Classify each sentence.

1. _____ Your name appeared below the picture of another person.

2. _____ Many noisy blackbirds gathered in our large oak tree.

Exercise 2: Use Sentence 2 to underline the complete subject once and the complete predicate twice and to complete the table below.

List the Noun Used	List the Noun Job	Singular or Plural	Common or Proper	Simple Subject	Simple Predicate
1.	2.	3.	4.	5.	6.
7.	8.	9.	10.		

Exercise 3: Name the six parts of speech that you have studied. (*You may use abbreviations.*)

1. _____ 2. _____ 3. _____ 4. _____ 5. _____ 6. _____

Exercise 4: Identify each pair of words as synonyms or antonyms by putting parentheses ( ) around **syn** or **ant**.

1. deep, shallow	syn ant	4. tardy, punctual	syn ant	7. gather, collect	syn ant
2. waddle, stride	syn ant	5. appear, emerge	syn ant	8. aware, alert	syn ant
3. beneath, below	syn ant	6. nimble, slow	syn ant	9. unsteady, stable	syn ant

Exercises 5: Correct the capitalization and punctuation mistakes. Write the rule numbers above the capitalization corrections and below the punctuation corrections. Use Reference 24 for the capitalization rules and Reference 26 for the punctuation rules. The references are located on pages 18 and 19 in your Reference Section.

_____ (capitalization rule numbers)

1. mr w r speer was born in denver colorado   (Editing Guide: 6 capitals & 5 punctuation)

_____ (punctuation rule numbers)

_____ (capitalization rule numbers)

2. mrs vines baked kelly a birthday cake on july 4 2002   (Editing Guide: 4 capitals & 3 punctuation)

_____ (punctuation rule numbers)

Exercise 6: In your journal, write a paragraph summarizing what you have learned this week.

Level 2—Shurley English—Homeschool Edition

Chapter 14 Test

Exercise 1: Classify each sentence.

1. _____ I climbed up the big hill yesterday.

2. _____ The three kittens sat lazily in their basket.

Exercise 2: Use Sentence 2 to underline the complete subject once and the complete predicate twice and to complete the table below.

List the Noun Used	List the Noun Job	Singular or Plural	Common or Proper	Simple Subject	Simple Predicate
1.	2.	3.	4.	5.	6.
7.	8.	9.	10.		

Exercise 3: Name the six parts of speech that you have studied. (*You may use abbreviations.*)

1. _____ 2. _____ 3. _____ 4. _____ 5. _____ 6. _____

Exercise 4: Identify each pair of words as synonyms or antonyms by putting parentheses ( ) around **syn** or **ant**.

1. counsel, advice	syn ant	4. collect, gather	syn ant	7. cranky, grouchy	syn ant
2. deep, shallow	syn ant	5. unsteady, stable	syn ant	8. burrow, tunnel	syn ant
3. senior, junior	syn ant	6. retire, begin	syn ant	9. appear, emerge	syn ant

Exercises 5: Correct the capitalization and punctuation mistakes. Write the rule numbers above the capitalization corrections and below the punctuation corrections. Use Reference 24 for the capitalization rules and Reference 26 for the punctuation rules. The references are located on pages 18 and 19 in your Reference Section.

_____ (capitalization rule numbers)

1. ray and judy moved to carson city nevada   (Editing Guide: 5 capitals & 2 punctuation)

_____ (punctuation rule numbers)

_____ (capitalization rule numbers)

2. mr and mrs davis were married on october 5 2001   (Editing Guide: 4 capitals & 4 punctuation)

_____ (punctuation rule numbers)

Exercise 6: In your journal, write a paragraph summarizing what you have learned this week.

Level 2—Shurley English—Homeschool Edition

Chapter 15 Test

Exercise 1: Classify each sentence.

1. _____ I went willingly to Susan's dance recital.

2. _____ My neighbor ate at my mom's new restaurant.

Exercise 2: Use Sentence 2 to underline the complete subject once and the complete predicate twice and to complete the table below.

List the Noun Used	List the Noun Job	Singular or Plural	Common or Proper	Simple Subject	Simple Predicate
1.	2.	3.	4.	5.	6.
7.	8.	9.	10.		

Exercise 3: Name the six parts of speech that you have studied. (*You may use abbreviations.*)

1. _____ 2. _____ 3. _____ 4. _____ 5. _____ 6. _____

Exercise 4: Identify each pair of words as synonyms or antonyms by putting parentheses ( ) around **syn** or **ant**.

1. burrow, tunnel	syn ant	4. senior, junior	syn ant	7. practice, rehearse	syn ant
2. crisp, soggy	syn ant	5. begin, retire	syn ant	8. contented, dissatisfied	syn ant
3. advice, counsel	syn ant	6. appear, emerge	syn ant	9. performance, recital	syn ant

Exercise 5: Use the following guidelines to make each noun possessive. First, identify each noun as singular or plural by writing **S** or **P** in the first blank. Next, write the correct rule number from the list below in the second blank. Finally, write the possessive form of each noun as singular possessive or as plural possessive.

1. For a singular noun - add (**'s**)	2. For a plural noun that ends in **s** - add (**'**)	3. For a plural noun that does not end in **s** - add (**'s**)
Rule 1: **girl's**	Rule 2: **girls'**	Rule 3: **women's**

Noun	S-P	Rule	Singular Possessive	Plural Possessive
1. bulbs				
2. jelly				
3. women				
4. Ben				
5. man				
6. knives				

Exercise 6: On notebook paper, write seven subject pronouns and seven possessive pronouns.

Exercise 7: In your journal, write a paragraph summarizing what you have learned this week.

Chapter 16 Test

Exercise 1: Classify each sentence.

1. _____ She looked sadly at the broken tree limbs in Grandmother's backyard.

2. _____ The kind babysitter smiled at the children's funny jokes.

Exercise 2: Use Sentence 1 to underline the complete subject once and the complete predicate twice and to complete the table below.

List the Noun Used	List the Noun Job	Singular or Plural	Common or Proper	Simple Subject	Simple Predicate
1.	2.	3.	4.	5.	6.
7.	8.	9.	10.		

Exercise 3: Name the six parts of speech that you have studied. (*You may use abbreviations.*)

1. _____ 2. _____ 3. _____ 4. _____ 5. _____ 6. _____

Exercise 4: Identify each pair of words as synonyms or antonyms by putting parentheses ( ) around **syn** or **ant**.

1. practice, rehearse	syn ant	4. crisp, soggy	syn ant	7. unexpected, awaited	syn ant
2. unsteady, stable	syn ant	5. middle, edge	syn ant	8. dissatisfied, contented	syn ant
3. favorite, preferred	syn ant	6. coast, shore	syn ant	9. performance, recital	syn ant

Exercise 5: Copy the following words on notebook paper. Write the correct contraction beside each word.
Words: is not, it is, are not, we are, was not, do not, did not, cannot, let us, I am, he is, who is, what is, were not.

Exercise 6: Copy the following contractions on notebook paper. Write the correct word beside each contraction.
Contractions: hasn't, couldn't, we'd, I'd, wouldn't, you'll, he'll, they'd, you'd, hadn't, they've, I've, she's.

Exercise 7: Use the following guidelines to make each noun possessive. First, identify each noun as singular or plural by writing **S** or **P** in the first blank. Next, write the correct rule number from the list below in the second blank. Finally, write the possessive form of each noun as singular possessive or as plural possessive.

1. For a singular noun - add ('s)	2. For a plural noun that ends in *s* - add (')		3. For a plural noun that does not end in *s* - add ('s)	
Rule 1: girl's	Rule 2: girls'		Rule 3: women's	
Noun	**S-P**	**Rule**	**Singular Possessive**	**Plural Possessive**
1. donut				
2. posters				
3. children				
4. Albert				

Exercise 8: In your journal, write a paragraph summarizing what you have learned this week.

Chapter 17 Test

Exercise 1: Classify each sentence.

1. _____ We sunned on the barren beach yesterday.

2. _____ My dad's new boat sails easily on the water.

Exercise 2: Use Sentence 2 to underline the complete subject once and the complete predicate twice and to complete the table below.

List the Noun Used	List the Noun Job	Singular or Plural	Common or Proper	Simple Subject	Simple Predicate
1.	2.	3.	4.	5.	6.
7.	8.	9.	10.		

Exercise 3: Identify each pair of words as synonyms or antonyms by putting parentheses ( ) around **syn** or **ant**.

1. coast, shore	syn ant	4. barren, desolate	syn ant	7. awaited, unexpected	syn ant
2. fresh, moldy	syn ant	5. edge, middle	syn ant	8. contented, dissatisfied	syn ant
3. enormous, huge	syn ant	6. effort, ease	syn ant	9. favorite, preferred	syn ant

Exercise 4: Copy the following words on notebook paper. Write the correct contraction beside each word.
Words: could not, you had, would not, she will, they would, he had, we have, she has, cannot, were not, you are, that is.

Exercise 5: Copy the following contractions on notebook paper. Write the correct word beside each contraction.
Contractions: shouldn't, she'd, they'll, he'll, we'd, hadn't, I've, let's, don't, you're, who's, isn't.

Exercise 6: Write the correct the answer for each sentence.
1. She won't share with me. _____
2. They are my neighbors. _____
3. We'd like to go with you. _____
4. They have bought a new car. _____

Exercise 7: Use the following guidelines to make each noun possessive. First, identify each noun as singular or plural by writing **S** or **P** in the first blank. Next, write the correct rule number from the list below in the second blank. Finally, write the possessive form of each noun as singular possessive or as plural possessive.

1. For a singular noun - add ('s)	2. For a plural noun that ends in *s* - add (')	3. For a plural noun that does not end in *s* - add ('s)
Rule 1: girl's	Rule 2: girls'	Rule 3: women's

Noun	S-P	Rule	Singular Possessive	Plural Possessive
1. ants				
2. Bob				
3. policemen				
4. reporter				

Exercise 8: In your journal, write a paragraph summarizing what you have learned this week.

Level 2—Shurley English—Homeschool Edition

Chapter 18 Test

Exercise 1: Classify each sentence.

1. _____ My baby brother ran toward the street in front of our house!

2. _____ They hid in their basement during the storm.

Exercise 2: Use Sentence 1 to underline the complete subject once and the complete predicate twice and to complete the table below.

List the Noun Used	List the Noun Job	Singular or Plural	Common or Proper	Simple Subject	Simple Predicate
1.	2.	3.	4.	5.	6.
7.	8.	9.	10.		
11.	12.	13.	14.		
15.	16.	17.	18.		

Exercise 3: Identify each pair of words as synonyms or antonyms by putting parentheses ( ) around *syn* or *ant*.

1. distant, remote	syn ant	4. effort, ease	syn ant	7. practice, rehearse	syn ant
2. barren, desolate	syn ant	5. restless, patient	syn ant	8. favorite, preferred	syn ant
3. narrow, wide	syn ant	6. enormous, huge	syn ant	9. arrogant, proud	syn ant

Exercise 4: On notebook paper, make each fragment below into a complete sentence. Underline the parts you add.

1. Add a subject part to this fragment: **tiptoed through the empty room**
2. Add a predicate part to this fragment: **The basketball team**

Exercise 5: Identify each kind of sentence by writing the abbreviation in the blank. (**S, F**)

_____ 1. The pretty yellow kitten.
_____ 2. The purple balloon floated in the breeze.
_____ 3. The young boy played the trumpet loudly.
_____ 4. Running quickly down the street.
_____ 5. The volcano erupted.

Exercise 6: Match each subject part with the correct predicate part by writing the correct sentence number in the blank.

Subject Parts		Predicate Parts
1. The choir members	_____	sizzled in the pan.
2. The pancake	_____	gave orders to the crew.
3. The ship's captain	_____	brought drinks to us.
4. My teacher	_____	sang in the church service.
5. Our waiter	_____	assigned math homework.

Exercise 7: In your journal, write a paragraph summarizing what you have learned this week.

Chapter 19 Test

Exercise 1: Classify each sentence.

1. _____ Arthur's brother lives on a deserted island.

2. _____ The stars sparkled brightly in the night.

Exercise 2: Use Sentence 2 to underline the complete subject once and the complete predicate twice and to complete the table below.

List the Noun Used	List the Noun Job	Singular or Plural	Common or Proper	Simple Subject	Simple Predicate
1.	2.	3.	4.	5.	6.
7.	8.	9.	10.		

Exercise 3: Identify each pair of words as synonyms or antonyms by putting parentheses ( ) around **syn** or **ant**.

1. remote, distant	syn ant	4. victory, defeat	syn ant	7. sparkle, shine	syn ant
2. shout, murmur	syn ant	5. narrow, wide	syn ant	8. arrogant, proud	syn ant
3. shelf, ledge	syn ant	6. moldy, fresh	syn ant	9. restless, patient	syn ant

Exercise 4: Use the following guidelines to make each noun possessive. First, identify each noun as singular or plural by writing **S** or **P** in the first blank. Next, write the correct rule number from the list below in the second blank. Finally, write the possessive form of each noun as singular possessive or as plural possessive.

1. For a singular noun - add (**'s**)	2. For a plural noun that ends in **s** - add (**'**)	3. For a plural noun that does not end in **s** - add (**'s**)
Rule 1: girl's	Rule 2: girls'	Rule 3: women's

Noun	S-P	Rule	Singular Possessive	Plural Possessive
1. horse				
2. men				
3. tractors				

Exercise 5: Match each subject part with the correct predicate part by writing the correct sentence number in the blank.

Subject Parts		Predicate Parts
1. The tea kettle	_____	burned in the toaster.
2. The juicy tomatoes	_____	flickered in the dark.
3. The crispy toast	_____	whistled loudly.
4. Several candles	_____	swayed in the wind.
5. The willow branches	_____	ripened on the vine.

Exercise 6: Copy the following words on notebook paper. Write the correct contraction beside each word.

<u>Words:</u> he would, you have, has not, do not, you are, who is, you had, they will, I will, will not, had not.

Exercise 7: In your journal, write a paragraph summarizing what you have learned this week.

Chapter 20 Test

Exercise 1: Classify each sentence.

1. _____ Andy's guitar fell into the murky waters of the pond.

2. _____ An injured whale swam beside the ship!

Exercise 2: Use Sentence 2 to underline the complete subject once and the complete predicate twice and to complete the table below.

List the Noun Used	List the Noun Job	Singular or Plural	Common or Proper	Simple Subject	Simple Predicate
1.	2.	3.	4.	5.	6.
7.	8.	9.	10.		

Exercise 3: Name the six parts of speech that you have studied. (*You may use abbreviations.*)

1. _____ 2. _____ 3. _____ 4. _____ 5. _____ 6. _____

Exercise 4: Identify each pair of words as synonyms or antonyms by putting parentheses ( ) around *syn* or *ant*.

1. ledge, shelf	syn ant	4. injure, damage	syn ant	7. shout, murmur	syn ant
2. depend, rely	syn ant	5. victory, defeat	syn ant	8. patient, restless	syn ant
3. anxious, relaxed	syn ant	6. sparkle, shine	syn ant	9. murky, clear	syn ant

Exercise 5: Identify the tense of each underlined verb by writing a number **1** for present tense, a number **2** for past tense, and a number **3** for future tense. Use the verb chart for the irregular verbs.

Verb Tense	Regular Verbs	Verb Tense	Irregular Verbs
	1. The pilot landed the plane.		9. The wind will blow against my window.
	2. The pilot lands the plane.		10. The wind blows against my window.
	3. The pilot will land the plane.		11. The wind blew against my window.
	4. Our pizza will cook in the oven.		12. The author wrote her second novel.
	5. Our pizza cooks in the oven.		13. The author will write her second novel.
	6. Our pizza cooked in the oven.		14. The author writes her second novel.
	7. My team scored a point.		15. My father wears his new suit.
	8. My team will score a point.		16. My father will wear his new suit.

Exercise 6: Copy the following words on notebook paper. Write the correct contraction beside each word.

Words: should not, I had, we will, will not, you would, had not, they have, has not, cannot, did not, we are, are not.

Exercise 7: In your journal, write a paragraph summarizing what you have learned this week.

Chapter 21 Test

Exercise 1: Classify each sentence.

1. _____ Bill ran swiftly to his house after school.

2. _____ The mother duck swam proudly around her ten ducklings.

Exercise 2: Use Sentence 1 to underline the complete subject once and the complete predicate twice and to complete the table below.

List the Noun Used	List the Noun Job	Singular or Plural	Common or Proper	Simple Subject	Simple Predicate
1.	2.	3.	4.	5.	6.
7.	8.	9.	10.		
11.	12.	13.	14.		

Exercise 3: Name the six parts of speech that you have studied. (*You may use abbreviations.*)

1. _____ 2. _____ 3. _____ 4. _____ 5. _____ 6. _____

Exercise 4: Identify each pair of words as synonyms or antonyms by putting parentheses ( ) around **syn** or **ant**.

1. depend, rely	syn ant	4. howl, whisper	syn ant	7. injure, damage	syn ant
2. frisky, lively	syn ant	5. clear, murky	syn ant	8. victory, defeat	syn ant
3. colorful, pale	syn ant	6. relaxed, anxious	syn ant	9. thrive, flourish	syn ant

Exercise 5: Identify the tense of each underlined verb by writing a number **1** for present tense, a number **2** for past tense, and a number **3** for future tense. Use the verb chart for the irregular verbs.

Verb Tense	Regular Verbs	Verb Tense	Irregular Verbs
	1. He grumbles about his chores.		8. Justin will bring the punch.
	2. He will grumble about his chores.		9. Justin brings the punch.
	3. He grumbled about his chores.		10. Justin brought the punch.
	4. I wrapped her gift.		11. The grass will grow in the spring.
	5. The candle glows in the darkness.		12. The grass grew in the spring.
	6. I will wrap her gift.		13. The snow falls softly to the ground.
	7. The candle glowed in the darkness.		14. The snow will fall softly to the ground.

Exercise 6: In your journal, write a paragraph summarizing what you have learned this week.

Chapter 22 Test

Exercise 1: Classify each sentence.

1. _____ Robert helped at his little brother's soccer game.

2. _____ The little bug landed lightly on Tim's nose.

Exercise 2: Use Sentence 2 to underline the complete subject once and the complete predicate twice and to complete the table below.

List the Noun Used	List the Noun Job	Singular or Plural	Common or Proper	Simple Subject	Simple Predicate
1.	2.	3.	4.	5.	6.
7.	8.	9.	10.		

Exercise 3: Identify each pair of words as synonyms or antonyms by putting parentheses ( ) around **syn** or **ant**.

1. inquire, question	syn ant	4. depend, rely	syn ant	7. thrive, flourish	syn ant
2. whisper, howl	syn ant	5. shrink, stretch	syn ant	8. thorough, meticulous	syn ant
3. lively, frisky	syn ant	6. rough, smooth	syn ant	9. colorful, pale	syn ant

Exercise 4: Write the parts of a friendly letter in the correct places in the friendly letter below.

1. **Heading**　　　2. **Greeting**　　　3. **Closing**　　　4. **Signature**
　　36 Ridge Road　　　　Dear Henry,　　　　Your friend,　　　　Wayne
　　Buffalo, NY 81800
　　March 16, 20___

5. **Body**
　　I got your letter yesterday. I can't wait for you to visit next month! Write soon.

Friendly Letter

Exercise 5: In your journal, write a paragraph summarizing what you have learned this week.

Level 2—Shurley English—Homeschool Edition

Chapter 23 Test

Exercise 1: Classify each sentence.

1. _____ The lost tourist waved to the policeman for his assistance.

2. _____ We stay with our grandmother after school.

Exercise 2: Use Sentence 2 to underline the complete subject once and the complete predicate twice and to complete the table below.

List the Noun Used	List the Noun Job	Singular or Plural	Common or Proper	Simple Subject	Simple Predicate
1.	2.	3.	4.	5.	6.
7.	8.	9.	10.		

Exercise 3: Name the six parts of speech that you have studied. *(You may use abbreviations.)*

1. _____ 2. _____ 3. _____ 4. _____ 5. _____ 6. _____

Exercise 4: Identify each pair of words as synonyms or antonyms by putting parentheses ( ) around **syn** or **ant**.

1. yearly, annual	syn ant	4. rough, smooth	syn ant	7. meticulous, thorough	syn ant
2. rowdy, gentle	syn ant	5. assistant, helper	syn ant	8. question, inquire	syn ant
3. thrive, flourish	syn ant	6. industrious, lazy	syn ant	9. stretch, shrink	syn ant

Exercise 5: Fill in the envelope with the parts provided. Draw a stamp in the proper place on the envelope.

Sample parts of an envelope:

1. Wayne Jones (writer)
   36 Ridge Road
   Buffalo, NY 81800

2. Henry Jackson (receiver)
   3445 Taylor Circle
   Fargo, ND 87200

Exercise 6: In your journal, write a paragraph summarizing what you have learned this week.

Level 2—Shurley English—Homeschool Edition

Chapter 24 Test

Exercise 1: Classify each sentence.

1. _____ The pig broke out of its pen yesterday.

2. _____ We stayed at our grandparents' house during the holidays.

Exercise 2: Use Sentence 2 to underline the complete subject once and the complete predicate twice and to complete the table below.

List the Noun Used	List the Noun Job	Singular or Plural	Common or Proper	Simple Subject	Simple Predicate
1.	2.	3.	4.	5.	6.
7.	8.	9.	10.		

Exercise 3: Name the six parts of speech that you have studied. (*You may use abbreviations.*)

1. _____ 2. _____ 3. _____ 4. _____ 5. _____ 6. _____

Exercise 4: Identify each pair of words as synonyms or antonyms by putting parentheses ( ) around **syn** or **ant**.

1. annual, yearly	syn ant	4. rowdy, gentle	syn ant	7. thorough, meticulous	syn ant
2. limp, hobble	syn ant	5. sweet, bitter	syn ant	8. lazy, industrious	syn ant
3. rude, polite	syn ant	6. assistant, helper	syn ant	9. continuous, ceaseless	syn ant

Exercises 5: Correct the capitalization and punctuation mistakes. Write the rule numbers above the capitalization corrections and below the punctuation corrections. Use Reference 24 for the capitalization rules and Reference 26 for the punctuation rules. The references are located on pages 18 and 19 in your Reference Section.

_____ (capitalization rule numbers)

i visited margaret in medford oregon   (Editing Guide: 4 capitals & 2 punctuation)

_____ (punctuation rule numbers)

Exercise 6: Write your own thank-you note. First, think of a person who has done something nice for you or has given you a gift (even the gift of time). Next, write that person a thank-you note, using the information in the Reference Section as a guide.

Exercise 7: In your journal, write a paragraph summarizing what you have learned this week.

Level 2—Shurley English—Homeschool Edition

Chapter 25 Test

Exercise 1: Classify each sentence.

1. _____ The exhausted eagle dropped slowly from the sky.

2. _____ Two small dogs barked loudly at the mailman's truck.

Exercise 2: Use Sentence 2 to underline the complete subject once and the complete predicate twice and to complete the table below.

List the Noun Used	List the Noun Job	Singular or Plural	Common or Proper	Simple Subject	Simple Predicate
1.	2.	3.	4.	5.	6.
7.	8.	9.	10.		

Exercise 3: Name the six parts of speech that you have studied. (*You may use abbreviations.*)

1. _____ 2. _____ 3. _____ 4. _____ 5. _____ 6. _____

Exercise 4: Identify each pair of words as synonyms or antonyms by putting parentheses ( ) around **syn** or **ant**.

1. hobble, limp	syn ant	4. thorough, meticulous	syn ant	7. shrink, stretch	syn ant
2. yearly, annual	syn ant	5. bitter, sweet	syn ant	8. whisper, howl	syn ant
3. polite, rude	syn ant	6. continuous, ceaseless	syn ant	9. industrious, lazy	syn ant

Exercise 5: Copy the following words on notebook paper. Write the correct contraction beside each word.
Words: we had, they will, will not, I would, have not, did not, we are, who is, I am, could not.

Exercise 5: Copy the following contractions on notebook paper. Write the correct word beside each contraction.
Contractions: shouldn't, I'd, he'll, she'd, we've, hasn't, don't, you're, that's, isn't.

Exercise 7: Underline the correct answer in each sentence.
1. Fiction books contain information and stories that are (**true, not true**).
2. Nonfiction books contain information and stories that are (**true, not true**).
3. The most common reference books are the dictionary and the encyclopedia. (**true, false**)

Exercise 8: In your journal, write a paragraph summarizing what you have learned this week.

Level 2—Shurley English—Homeschool Edition

Chapter 26 Test

Exercise 1: Classify each sentence.

1. _____ The science students experimented frequently in their new laboratory during the holidays.

2. _____ Jamie's computer mouse moved smoothly over the new pad.

Exercise 2: Use Sentence 1 to underline the complete subject once and the complete predicate twice and to complete the table below.

List the Noun Used	List the Noun Job	Singular or Plural	Common or Proper	Simple Subject	Simple Predicate
1.	2.	3.	4.	5.	6.
7.	8.	9.	10.		
11.	12.	13.	14.		

Exercise 3: Identify each pair of words as synonyms or antonyms by putting parentheses ( ) around **syn** or **ant**.

1. rude, polite	syn ant	4. assistant, helper	syn ant	7. continuous, ceaseless	syn ant
2. rowdy, gentle	syn ant	5. bitter, sweet	syn ant	8. yearly, annual	syn ant
3. limp, hobble	syn ant	6. whisper, howl	syn ant	9. lazy, industrious	syn ant

Exercise 4: Match each part of a book listed below with the type of information it may give you. Write the appropriate letter in the blank. You may use each letter only once.

A. Title Page   B. Index   C. Appendix   D. Bibliography   E. Body   F. Preface   G. Copyright page

1. _____ Exact page numbers for a particular topic and used to locate topics quickly

2. _____ Text of the book

3. _____ Reason the book was written

4. _____ Books listed for finding more information

5. _____ ISBN number

6. _____ Publisher's name and city where the book was published

7. _____ Extra maps in a book

Exercise 5: On notebook paper, write the five parts found at the front of a book.

Exercise 6: On notebook paper, write the four parts found at the back of a book.

Exercise 7: In your journal, write a paragraph summarizing what you have learned this week.

Level 2—Shurley English—Homeschool Edition

Chapter 27 Test

Exercise 1: Classify each sentence.

1. _____ Paul's brother fell into a muddy ditch behind the playground.

2. _____ The sun shines brightly through my bedroom window.

Exercise 2: Use Sentence 1 to underline the complete subject once and the complete predicate twice and to complete the table below.

List the Noun Used	List the Noun Job	Singular or Plural	Common or Proper	Simple Subject	Simple Predicate
1.	2.	3.	4.	5.	6.
7.	8.	9.	10.		
11.	12.	13.	14.		

Exercise 3: Underline the correct homonym in each sentence.
1. (Their, There) are five players on the court.
2. (It's, Its) time for dinner.
3. Does (your, you're) toy need batteries?
4. (Here, Hear) is my watch!
5. Can we go (to, too, two) the store?
6. (Right, Write) your name on your paper.

Exercise 4: For each sentence, do these four things: (1) Write the subject. (2) Write **S** if the subject is singular or **P** if the subject is plural. (3) Write the rule number. (4) Underline the correct verb in the sentence.

Rule 1 and Rule 2 are located in Reference 21 on page 17 in your student book.

Subject	S or P	Rule	
			1. Violets (blooms, bloom) in the flowerbed.
			2. Tommy (work, works) during the summer.
			3. The mozzarella cheese (melts, melt) on the pizza.
			4. The soldiers (stands, stand) in straight lines.
			5. The fog (float, floats) across the lake.
			6. You (combs, comb) your hair.
			7. The city counsel members (meet, meets) next door.
			8. Her math book (weigh, weighs) five pounds.
			9. Joseph (stand, stands) next to Jennifer.

Exercise 5: In your journal, write a paragraph summarizing what you have learned this week.

SENTENCE

SECTION

DIRECTIONS FOR THE SENTENCE TIME SECTION:

Use colored markers to match each label with the correct sentence part by drawing a line from one to the other. Then, use the labels to arrange the sentence parts into a sentence that you will write on the sentence line below. *(The order of the words in your sentence should be in the same sequence as the vertical list of labels.)* Create other labels and scrambled sentence parts on notebook paper for family members to solve. You may color code the sentence parts.

Chapter 2, Lesson 5, Sentence: Sentence Time directions are located above.	
Labels for Order of Sentence	**Scrambled Sentence Parts**
SN	howled
V	coyotes
Sentence:	

Chapter 3, Lesson 5, Sentence: Sentence Time directions are located above.	
Labels for Order of Sentence	**Scrambled Sentence Parts**
Adj	today
Adj	landed
SN	jumbo
V	jets
Adv	big
Adv	safely
Sentence:	

Chapter 4, Lesson 4, Sentence: Sentence Time directions are located above.	
Labels for Order of Sentence	**Scrambled Sentence Parts**
A	ran
Adj	the
Adj	yesterday
SN	shiny
V	perfectly
Adv	engine
Adv	new
Sentence:	

Chapter 5, Lesson 4, Sentence: Sentence Time directions are located on page 109.

Labels for Order of Sentence	Scrambled Sentence Parts
A	squirrel
Adj	loudly
Adj	a
SN	complained
V	grumpy
Adv	old

Sentence:

Chapter 6, Lesson 4, Sentence: Sentence Time directions are located on page 109.

Labels for Order of Sentence	Scrambled Sentence Parts
A	young
Adj	today
SN	the
V	excitedly
Adv	whispered
Adv	children

Sentence:

Chapter 7, Lesson 4, Sentence: Sentence Time directions are located on page 109.

Labels for Order of Sentence	Scrambled Sentence Parts
A	silently
Adj	eagle
SN	overhead
V	the
Adv	flew
Adv	magnificent

Sentence:

Chapter 8, Lesson 5, Sentence: Sentence Time directions are located on page 109.	
Labels for Order of Sentence	**Scrambled Sentence Parts**
A	children
Adj	performed
SN	funny
V	the
P	clowns
A	for
OP	the

Sentence:

Chapter 9, Lesson 5, Sentence: Sentence Time directions are located on page 109.	
Labels for Order of Sentence	**Scrambled Sentence Parts**
A	huge
SN	in
V	family
P	mall
A	shopped
Adj	the
OP	the

Sentence:

Chapter 10, Lesson 5, Sentence: Sentence Time directions are located on page 109.	
Labels for Order of Sentence	**Scrambled Sentence Parts**
A	along
Adj	garden
Adj	hopped
SN	a
V	the
P	edge
A	rabbit
OP	brown
P	of
A	curious
OP	the

Sentence:

Level 2—Shurley English—Homeschool Edition

Chapter 11, Lesson 4, Sentence: Sentence Time directions for independent work are given by the teacher.	
Labels for Order of Sentence	**Scrambled Sentence Parts**
Independent sentence assignment.	

Chapter 12, Lesson 5, Sentence: Sentence Time directions are located on page 109.	
Labels for Order of Sentence	**Scrambled Sentence Parts**
SP	along
V	quietly
Adv	the
P	walked
A	path
Adj	in
OP	lovely
P	city
A	the
Adj	we
OP	park
Sentence:	

Chapter 13, Lesson 5, Sentence: Sentence Time directions are located on page 109.	
Labels for Order of Sentence	**Scrambled Sentence Parts**
SP	outside
V	snow
Adv	the
P	in
A	we
OP	new
P	neighbors
PP	our
Adj	with
OP	played
Sentence:	

Chapter 14, Lesson 5, Sentence: Sentence Time directions are located on page 109.

Labels for Order of Sentence	Scrambled Sentence Parts
A	rain
Adj	the
SN	heavy
V	after
P	appeared
A	beautiful
OP	sky
P	the
A	rainbow
Adj	across
OP	a

Sentence:

Chapter 15, Lesson 5, Sentence: Sentence Time directions are located on page 109.

Labels for Order of Sentence	Scrambled Sentence Parts
SP	Grandmother's
V	for
Adv	arrival
P	we
PN	anxiously
OP	after
P	waited
A	snowstorm
OP	the

Sentence:

Chapter 16, Lesson 5, Sentence: Sentence Time directions are located on page 109.

Labels for Order of Sentence	Scrambled Sentence Parts
PP	belonged
Adj	friend
SN	brother's
V	our
P	my
PP	to
PN	puppy
OP	new

Sentence:

Chapter 17, Lesson 5, Sentence: Sentence Time directions are located on page 109.	
Labels for Order of Sentence	**Scrambled Sentence Parts**
A	wildly
SN	team
V	quarterback's
Adv	fans
P	touchdown
PP	the
OP	for
P	after
A	yelled
PN	their
Adj	the
OP	outstanding

Sentence:

Chapter 18, Lesson 5, Sentence: Sentence Time directions are located on page 109.	
Labels for Order of Sentence	**Scrambled Sentence Parts**
PP	mother
SN	children's
V	laughter
P	playtime
PP	my
PN	her
OP	their
P	at
PP	during
OP	smiled

Sentence:

Chapter 19, Lesson 5, Sentence: Sentence Time directions are located on page 109.	
Labels for Order of Sentence	**Scrambled Sentence Parts**
PP	frantically
PN	today
SN	my
V	her
Adv	sister's
P	for
PP	looked
Adj	ring
OP	friend
Adv	diamond

Sentence:

Chapter 20, Lesson 5, Sentence: Sentence Time directions are located on page 109.	
Labels for Order of Sentence	**Scrambled Sentence Parts**
A	in
SN	during
P	the
A	the
OP	the
V	wood
Adv	fireplace
P	day
A	brightly
Adj	cold
Adj	burned
OP	winter

Sentence:

Chapter 21, Lesson 5, Sentence: Sentence Time directions for independent work are given by the teacher.	
Labels for Order of Sentence	**Scrambled Sentence Parts**
Independent sentence assignment.	

Chapter 22, Lesson 5, Sentence: Sentence Time directions are located on page 109.	
Labels for Order of Sentence	**Scrambled Sentence Parts**
PP	to
PN	new
SN	cousin's
V	the
P	his
A	elementary
Adj	yesterday
Adj	neighbor
OP	school
Adv	walked
Sentence:	

Chapter 23, Lesson 5, Sentence: Sentence Time directions are located on page 109.	
Labels for Order of Sentence	**Scrambled Sentence Parts**
A	snow
Adj	in
Adj	their
SN	yellow
V	the
P	for
A	pecked
OP	food
P	the
PP	pretty
OP	birds
Sentence:	

Chapter 24, Lesson 5, Sentence: Sentence Time directions are located on page 109.

Labels for Order of Sentence	Scrambled Sentence Parts
SP	at
V	during
P	joke
PP	time
Adj	family
PN	funny
Adj	brother's
OP	I
P	my
Adj	laughed
OP	big

Sentence:

Chapter 25, Lesson 5, Sentence: Sentence Time directions are located on page 109.

Labels for Order of Sentence	Scrambled Sentence Parts
PP	my
Adj	my
SN	garden
V	new
P	prize-winning
PP	dug
PN	neighbor's
Adj	in
Adj	puppy
OP	flower

Sentence:

Chapter 26, Lesson 5, Sentence: Sentence Time directions are located on page 109.

Labels for Order of Sentence	Scrambled Sentence Parts
SP	swiftly
V	recess
Adv	swings
P	we
A	to
OP	ran
P	the
OP	during

Sentence:

Chapter 27, Lesson 5, Sentence: Sentence Time directions are located on page 109.

Labels for Order of Sentence	Scrambled Sentence Parts
A	the
Adj	the
SN	the
V	at
Adv	on
P	hungry
A	chocolate
Adj	longingly
OP	counter
P	boys
A	cake
OP	stared

Sentence: